It Just Happens To Be Gluten-Free

By Jen Fiore

ISBN: 979-8-218-24872-7

First edition October 2023.
Location of publication.

Published by Do Life Inspired Publishing

Book Design by Michaela Keil
www.michaelakeil.com

For information about custom editions, special sales,
corporate purchases, interviews and guest appearances with
Jen Fiore, please email dolifeinspired@gmail.com

I dedicate this book to my family. My mom and dad who taught me cooking basics and showed me the value of our nightly family dinners. My husband and children gave me a purpose for one of my great passions. Thank you all for helping me get to this moment where I can share something I love and make it such an intricate part of my joy-filled life!

Table of Contents

Starters & Sides

Soups and Salads

Breads

Mains

Desserts

About The Author

Food and Family

Each of my family members has shaped my life in a powerful way, and their influence extends to my love of food. My husband has been my supporter since the moment we fell in love — from that first tuna casserole I made for him in my parent's kitchen while we were dating and through the years. There is nothing I can't do in his eyes, and he makes me see the potential in myself when I lose sight of it. Again, that includes food. He believes that what I come up with in my kitchen will be far better than anything at a restaurant, and he is willing to bank money on it!

My mother was my very first source of encouragement in the kitchen.

I will always remember the first dish I created for my dad with the variety of ingredients she let me play around with. It was obvious that it was not going to be something fabulous. She set me up with my apron and let me smoosh bread in milk and season with herbs, but to that three-year-old child, I was putting all my love into something for someone I loved dearly.

My father! His joyous personality helped to cultivate within me a love for life, family, and all things food! He showed me how food can help create comradery with others. There wasn't any type of food or experience my father didn't encourage me to embrace. His passion for life and food has been greatly missed these last 20 years. He is forever in our hearts and minds.

I express my love for my family each day through food. Having three kids with Celiac disease, as well as myself, in a time when nothing was available at the grocery store was a challenge. I had to learn cooking and baking in a new way. But as I did play and create, I watched my children's happiness in enjoying meals at home. Getting excited about a new dish was commonplace. It brought me so much pleasure to watch the children get excited as I created food for them! I would think back to my own childhood and say to myself, "I don't want these kids to miss out on any celebration because of food and dietary restrictions. I want them to create memories and traditions that they can carry to their own family when the time comes." I am so full of gratitude and love that this was exactly what our experience was.

Introduction

Food is an experience — an immersive journey through the taste, smell, and look of a dish. Food is a welcomed partner in friendship, in family, and in celebration: Cooking or baking is an expression of love. It is the ever-present guest at every life event. From weddings to end-of-life celebrations, special dinners for a job well done to 50th wedding anniversaries, food is an expression of how much we care. It is the balm that can calm a soul and warm a heart. Its role in life is to nurture both the body and the spirit. For many, food is a valued part of one's life, like a friend who has stuck with you for ages — knowing exactly what you need and when.

When I was growing up, we didn't call ourselves "foodies;" we called ourselves Italians.

I have such fond memories of family gatherings, laughing and joking while several conversations were happening at the same time. No matter the event we were celebrating, delicious food was always center stage. In time, I realized that my family was not the only one to experience this relationship with food. It was not just us Italians! Throughout the years, I've watched so many families honor their heritage and traditions through food. I saw important days marked by their favorite dish. I saw smiles and happiness when they remembered the meal they made or shared a story about who made the best dessert.

My food journey began in New York. I was raised in an Italian-American family (both sets of grandparents were born in Italy, so my parents were the first Americans in our family). My grandparents took Sunday dinner very seriously; meaning, we couldn't be late to the table, and there was a tremendous amount of food, just in case every person at the table wanted a second serving or on the off chance 5-8 other people were going to drop by. At a very young age, I knew the importance food played in our lives, and it went way beyond nurturing our body.

What I witnessed was pure joy! Whoever hosted Sunday dinner used food as a major part of the celebration. Throughout my entire childhood, I felt love in every bite. Food was an expression of my mom and dad's family heritage (Sicilian and Neapolitan), coupled with a desire to make those at the table happy. Another part of the joy experienced was from the actual taste of these delicious dishes that were created.

However, dinners weren't always easy. Since the age of eight, I suffered tremendous stomach pain and distress, which is just a nice way of saying that most of the time, I would have to rush to the bathroom after I ate. We searched for an answer to this mysterious illness that would sometimes last for days on end, but other times would give me a reprieve. There was never any rhyme or reason, so I just had to learn to cope with it. The doctors were mystified. I was resolved to truck on through life and enjoy it the best I could when I could. Although my chief complaints were stomach-related, food was still a great love of mine; I just didn't know why it didn't like me back.

In 2003, I discovered the answer to this lifelong battle with stomach illness (and so many more symptoms that I gathered in the 27 years) was an auto-immune disease called Celiac disease. I also learned, shortly after, that our three children, who were suffering much the same as I did, had the same disease. The cure for such a disease? A strict gluten-free diet.

Eureka! We had an answer to decades of prayers, pain, and tears. My brain started rattling off all that would now happen in my life: more energy, no more pain in my bones, no more stomach distress, no more hospital visits. I just couldn't contain my joy! Then my brain also reminded me, "What the heck is gluten?"

As you may recall, 2003 was a time when there wasn't anything at the grocery store that had the strange words "gluten-free" on the packaging. I wasn't the only person clueless about gluten. I had to learn how to feed myself and the kids. I had to read labels. I had to learn how to bake! Yikes! I was a cook through and through, but baking was nowhere in my wheelhouse.

I thought about my childhood and my love of the food my family made, about the family gatherings and big parties with huge menus, about the role that food plays in our life and our love. I thought, "Why should anyone miss out on any life experience because of food?" How the heck was I going to feed people my food, celebrate as big as I always had, and have everything taste the same as food with gluten in it?

I cried in the closet. I didn't want the kids to feel defeated like I felt. Then I realized I needed to step up and control this narrative!

I became "Vigilante Mom" with an invisible cape as I attacked every single recipe and tried to make them gluten-free...and edible. I had so much to learn about this new lifestyle, and I took our health very seriously. I was hyper-aware of every situation where the kids would be exposed to food. In a calm-and-controlled manner, I took over. It was so much easier to take control of their food prep and intake rather than risk their wellness. In order to do this (cue in scary music), I had to learn how to bake. I researched where to find gluten-free food and ingredients. I was determined to give our children a wonderful childhood, full of fun and comradery like before the diagnosis. I didn't want them to have any negative focus on what they couldn't have, but rather to celebrate that they could still have everything — it was now just homemade. I wanted them to have a cupcake when the other kids were celebrating their birthdays in school. (Side note: You do not realize how often there are celebrations and treats in school until you have to bake something similar to what is being provided and then do that times three!) I also wanted people to come to our home and still enjoy the food prepared as they always had.

I played in the kitchen. In the beginning, it was a crapshoot, but I just kept plugging along because I knew of no other options. I watched my kids grow into people who appreciate homemade food in the spirit of the love in which it was made. They showed their gratitude from an early age, thanking me for baking their treats and then thanking me for making their Christmas (or whichever celebrations) so special. We forged some amazing family traditions as a result of our diagnosis. Our kids grew to be adults who not only continued their gratitude for food but also were appreciative of where the food came from and how it nurtured their bodies and how certain foods were better for their wellness.

You, too, will see that your efforts are appreciated. Whoever you are cooking and baking for will love that you are playing around in the kitchen for them! I highly recommend that you adopt a judgment-free zone in your cooking space. I remember the first cake that fell, or when I took a cake out of the pan too soon and it crumbled, or the times I forgot to add salt to bread recipes. In all these instances, I readjusted. I made cake pops out of the crumbled cake or deliciously seasoned croutons from the unsalted bread. But most importantly, I stopped judging my efforts in the kitchen. Nothing is a lost venture!

This cookbook contains some of our recipes from our 20 years of baking and cooking gluten-free because, let's face it, each one of us in this family has our favorite things. After all, we are from a long line of foodies.

Food has continued to remain, as I always hoped it would, an extension of love. It was once my way to show the kids that they could live a normal life with their gluten-free food and be healthy at the same time. I worked to unlock some key dishes that our kids wanted to share with our gluten-eating friends and family. Eventually, the hard work paid off and people started asking me for my recipes. My son suggested I create a YouTube channel to share the recipes rather than having to email everyone who asked. So, I did. And when I owned a restaurant for five years, I saw need to offer gluten-free sandwiches and salads not only to my own family but also to the community. I wanted to show that gluten-free food is delicious and do it on local T.V.; so I do that, too.

I wanted to write this cookbook to help others get comfortable in the kitchen and enjoy the recipes my family enjoys. I hope through this cookbook and my story you can take a literal page from my book and focus more on the energy of providing a meal made from love, rather than if it is worthy of a social media post. I cannot express how many creations I have made when I jokingly stated, "Close your eyes and take a bite! You won't be disappointed!" I knew the taste was there, even if I hadn't mastered the appearance just yet. After all, I am a real person. I may not be classically trained, but out of love and then necessity, I learned.

I had a feeling that even gluten-eaters would enjoy these dishes. I would serve them food and watch their reactions as I would state:

"IT JUST HAPPENS TO BE GLUTEN-FREE!"

Jen's Kitchen Notes

My Thoughts on Servings

I debated on the topic of serving sizes for this cookbook. How can I tell you what a serving size is for your family? I believe that serving sizes are family-specific. Heck, even person-specific! As I created dishes, I would keep in mind which dishes would make delicious leftovers and which ones were always better freshly made. If you keep these factors in mind, along with the size of the baking/cooking dish or pan I recommended that you use, then you can visualize what your servings will look like.

Little Tweaks Make a Huge Difference

You may notice that nearly every recipe has a space labeled "Tweaks." I included this section so you could write down your notes or adjustments for the recipe. Remember, every creation is your extension of love to your friends, family, and guests as well as your preferences. I am hoping that you are encouraged to experiment and branch out in the kitchen to make each recipe your own. I think of food as more than just a means to an end — cooking, baking, and sharing are part of the joy of eating.

Food fuels our bodies and can be used as medicine! Depending on the ingredients, the benefits can last well after the meal is done. You can take your food wherever you want to! You can create dishes focusing on the importance of digestion, asking, "What can my body use efficiently?" You can address what foods are GMO, which foods are rich in fiber, which vegetables have the most minerals, smoke points of different oils, removing refined sugar, finding flours packed with nutrients, which meals are low in carbohydrates, or which are high in healthy fats. The list of adjustments and tweaks goes on and on, giving us so many wonderful opportunities for delicious food that is good for our bodies.

But it can be easy to fall down a rabbit hole while trying to make healthier choices because there are so many things that you can address. Rather than get overwhelmed, I suggest you address one piece at a time. You can still make tweaks to recipes or remove certain items from your kitchen that you learned may be harmful, just tackle one thing at a time. For example, many years ago, I read about the danger of consuming too much aluminum. I thought "Gosh, I use aluminum all the time, how will I tackle that?" Rather than throwing everything out, I reduced our use of aluminum foil. If I was BBQing, I would wrap the fish in parchment first then in foil to withstand the grill. Cookies bake great on a parchment-lined baking sheet. You can even find silicone baking tools or glass dishes. When you tackle one thing at a time, it doesn't become overwhelming. And in time, all the little changes make a big difference when added together.

Little tweaks here and there help make a big shift!

Ingredients

As you read through these recipes, you'll notice that some ingredients are specific. Here is what I use and why. Knowing why one version of an ingredient is used over another is a good way to learn how you may want to tweak the ingredients in your version of the recipe!

Salt: I like to use Himalayan salt when I can. It brings a tad more salt to a dish. If I don't want the coarse texture or pink tinge, then I use sea salt.

Olive Oil: I only use extra virgin olive oil because it is the least processed of the olive oils and retains most of the vitamins and antioxidants. When a recipe calls for olive oil, please feel free to substitute it with whatever olive oil you prefer (see What's The Deal With Olive Oil?, page 21).

Garlic Powder: Many of my recipes use fine garlic powder. I like to use this type of garlic powder for its smooth texture in the recipes. If you have granulated garlic on hand, feel free to use that but know its texture is slightly more coarse and sandy than the fine powder.

Sugar: I like to use unrefined sugar or raw cane sugar in my recipes. If I want a bit of molasses flavor, I use turbinado, which is minimally processed and refined.

Garlic

We love garlic around here! There is no such thing as too much in my opinion. All joking aside, I understand my opinion is simply that, an opinion. Perhaps you like less garlic in your recipes. Make the adjustments to my recipes and don't forget to jot down the amount you preferred in the "Tweaks" section for the next time.

I'd love to share a few facts about fresh garlic that could change your mind about adding more of it to your life and your recipes. Many studies have shown that Allium sativum L. (the scientific name for garlic) has antioxidant, antimicrobial, anti-inflammatory, and even anti-cancer properties. Some studies show that it can even improve cardiovascular health and help with immunity.

There is a concoction that I make and affectionately named my Magic Elixir. I use it to address inflammation in my body, to knock out a headache, and even to help with the flora in the intestines! Think of all the benefits you can get from one drink that has fresh garlic!

MAGIC ELIXIR

1 cup filtered water
2 Tbsp raw apple cider vinegar
2 Tbsp fresh lemon juice
1 fresh garlic clove, grated
1" (or 1 Tbsp) fresh ginger, grated

Add together into a glass cup or jar and mix. I like to add a few drops of Stevia before drinking. I suggest you drink it down as soon as you make it to get all the benefits of these fresh ingredients.

There are lots of ways to use garlic: in a drink, roasted in the oven as a snack, sautéd for a dish, to flavor olive oil, or as an herbal tincture. If you are interested in getting the health benefits of this little vegetable but don't adore the taste as much as me, then you can use it in herbal forms, such as pills or tinctures.

A Bit About Fats

When baking, you can branch out and use other fats that aren't butter. I like to tweak a recipe using healthier substitutions while still achieving a good flavor. I usually choose olive oil, ghee, avocado oil, or coconut oil when I am playing around with a recipe. They each have a unique footprint they leave behind in a recipe, so keep in mind the flavors of the fat you substitute with. Certain oils can have savory notes. Also, keep in mind how oil responds in the recipe differently than butter when you are making "tweaks." In some recipes, it's divine! For every cup of solid fat replaced, use ¾ cup of liquid fat.

Coconut oil is a great healthier fat you can use as a substitute for butter in many vegan recipes. With its hint of coconut flavor, it adds a wonderful complex nuttiness to your recipe. Other solid fats, which bring lift and creaminess to a recipe, are margarine, shortening, and lard.

If a recipe calls for a solid fat (which will cream together with sugar to create lovely air pockets), I might try another solid fat. Or, I might go rogue and replace the solid fat with an oil with a pinch of psyllium husk powder. If I replace a solid fat with a liquid fat, I might also increase the amount of baking powder to create more levity! The key things I keep in mind when tweaking a recipe are that the "tweak" may add a healthy benefit and that it will maintain a great flavor!

There are a great number of fats you can use in cooking. In my recipes, I stick to a few of my tried-and-true friends. I am not suggesting you cannot use the oil or fat you want; of course, you can, but I have shared here the ones I like that work best with these recipes.

The list of oils you can use in cooking is lengthy. There are books on fats alone! I would suggest you keep a few factors in mind when choosing your fats if you would like to "tweak" the recipes: what are the needs of my family (i.e. health or dietary restrictions), taste, what the fat is being used for (cooking, frying, drizzle/dressing), smoke points, saturated (saturated fats commonly used in cooking are coconut oil, ghee, lard, and palm oil), and unsaturated (unsaturated fats commonly used in cooking are vegetable oils, such as flaxseed oil, canola oil, olive oil, sesame oil, peanut oil, and avocado oil), and which is best to use in which way.

Organic, Hormone-Free, and Antibiotic-Free. Oh My!

When the kids were growing up, I tried to maintain a general rule when purchasing groceries, "Do the best you can!" In our health journey as a family, I would buy our main staples — milk, eggs, chicken, apples, pears, broccoli, and spinach — all organic, free of hormones and antibiotics. If my weekly budget allowed, I would buy other organic items as well. Buying gluten-free flours, snacks, and more have always been more costly than their gluten counterparts, and years ago, a lot of my food budget was spent on the small market of gluten-free options. I did the best I could to get healthy, fresh food for the family. Sometimes the local supermarket didn't have organic, so I had no choice. I researched which vegetables and fruit were okay to purchase non-organic over others, then I would wash everything in a mixture of 3 parts water + 1 part distilled white vinegar. I'd spray or soak for 5 minutes, then rinse and pat dry and then place in the refrigerator or use. I tried the best I could and didn't judge myself when I couldn't buy everything organic.

What's The Deal With Olive Oil?

Extra virgin olive oil (EVOO) is my favorite! I use it whenever I can for its nutty, savory taste but also its medicinal benefit. High-quality olive oil can make a difference in a meal, but not every olive oil is created the same.

Virgin olive oil (VOO) has been extracted from olives mechanically. Extra virgin is a grade of virgin. Purchasing olive oil can be a bit confusing because each company is telling you why they are the best. Olive oils are naturally higher in oleic acid (omega-9 fatty acid that helps prevent heart disease and reduces cholesterol).

Perhaps keeping in mind what you are needing from the oil would help in the selection process. If you read the label, it should tell you how it was processed. EVOO oil is cold-pressed, or unrefined, and graded only as extra-virgin if it has no defects and has a free acidy that is less than or equal to 0.8 (as per the National Olive Oil Association).

Certifying that oil is extra virgin is a long process, which may contribute to its higher cost. It may have a heavier fruity or nutty flavor. Some people said that it has a pepper taste, herbal flavor, or even a spicy note. VOO is a grade below extra virgin with a free acidity of 0.8-2.0.

If the oil is labeled as just "olive oil," then it was simply refined. It has been processed more to remove impurities and have a milder, more subtle taste.

EVOO or VOO have more medicinal properties: more nutrients, vitamins, and polyphenols. Polyphenols are a category of compounds; they have anti-inflammatory properties that help reduce chronic illness and are naturally found in plant foods, such as fruits, vegetables, herbs, spices, teas, dark chocolate, and wine.

Olive oil has been said to be good for cardiovascular health and helps to reduce the risk of cancer and other degenerative diseases. I try to add nutrient-rich, polyphenol-rich items to every meal. The antioxidant and anti-inflammatory benefits are a goal I personally try to keep in mind when cooking for myself.

I take full advantage of the high polyphenol count in EVOO — and the great taste! I take ½ Tbsp of my high-quality EVOO daily. I drink it right down the hatch, or I use it generously as a drizzle or make salad dressing with it. I use it because I love the taste and also to lower the inflammation in my body due to degenerative arthritis, lower high cholesterol, help with memory, help prevent diabetes, and lower blood pressure, too.

With a small amount of research, you can find the olive oil that works best for your cooking needs and your health!

Not Every Egg Can Be Trusted

Crack your eggs into a bowl instead of straight into your recipe. The worst thing is to waste your ingredients on a rotten egg! It is a shame to waste the ingredients, the cost of the ingredients, and your time!

Pour Don't Scoop

Many baking recipes list the ingredients by weight. Most of my recipes in this cookbook (excluding my sourdough bread) use volumetric measurements, so accuracy here matters. Sticking a measuring cup into a bag of flour tends to pack in the flour, which isn't the best for baking. I place my measuring cup on a dish and pour the flour into it, or I take a spoon and spoon the flour into the cup — NO packing down the flour at any point. Then I take the flat edge of a butter knife or spatula and scrape the excess off the top. The remaining flour in the dish gets placed back into the flour container.

Mark The Date

Whether you are placing your flours in an airtight container (which I adore doing because it makes the pantry so much more organized and grabbing the flours I need easier) or leaving them in their original bags. Whatever method you use, mark the date on the open bag. You can use a sticker label on the container or a dry-erase marker, and if you are keeping the flour in a bag, place a sticky note or marker the date right on there. I stick by a loose rule of six months for a flour's freshness. Plopping a date on things helps to let you know when your flour is coming close to that mark, then you can use it soon rather than losing it!

Lists Make The World Go Round

I am a big list chick! I love a list in my pantry, fridge, and deep freezer. Why so many lists, you ask? To make life easier, of course! Here are the lists I like to keep and where:

Time To Order: I keep a list on the decorative basket that holds my flour bags and extras. I keep my airtight containers of flours on a shelf, and just below them, I always have the backup flours. I keep a list of the flour in each basket. When I take from the basket to refill a container, I know exactly when that flour needs to go on the "Need To Order" list!

The "Need To Order" List: Most people have a grocery list they have begun somewhere in their kitchen or on a phone app. I have a grocery list and an online ordering list. I cannot get the gluten-free flours I use at our local grocery stores, so I have to hit the web! I keep this list right alongside the grocery list in a small ceramic basket hanging outside of the pantry. It is the location everyone knows to go to once they have eaten the last of something. Nothing worse than not knowing when you need to get a well-loved item because no one let you know it was low or even worse...gone!

Deep Freezing Is Your Friend — Not Foe: When the kids were younger, I used our deep freezer like a dear friend. At all times, the kids and my husband would know what was in there with very little effort. I hung a corkboard and tacked one list for frozen foods to cook, one list for frozen foods I baked, and one list for the sweets/snack on the shelves across from the freezer. (I had the freezer in the walk-in pantry). When someone used an item from the freezer, they were asked to put a line through it (I had a pen hanging from the corkboard).

Big Box Stores Need Dates: When you shop at a big box store and get lots of items, I highly recommend writing yourself a list of dates for the perishable items. The reason to shop in bulk is the price savings, but there is nothing worse than when the broccoli goes bad because you forgot the date, or the chicken smells and you are worrying whether you should cook it or not! For these big-haul purchases, I suggest a small dry-erase board that can be kept on the side of the fridge that can also list meal prep for the week. Take into consideration the dates of the items, and prepare your meal plan around those items to ensure you use them before you lose them!

Playing With Bread!

You can leave your fresh bread on the counter for a couple of days, but to make the most of your baking efforts, use that freezer as your friend. I promise it will be so much better than any store-bought frozen bread. Put parchment or wax paper in between the slices and mark the bag with the date. Take a slice out one hour before it's needed for lunch time, or toast it and enjoy your creation.

Want to play around with different flours? Perhaps you want a loaf of bread with more protein or fiber? I would highly recommend switching things up and having fun. Be adventurous!

While playing with the bread recipes, keep the following "general" rules in mind to help you make some delicious loaves and possibly uncover your new favorite!

#1: Keep the starch in your bread at about ⅓ of the total in the flour portion of the recipe (i.e. 1 cup of starch with 2 cups of protein flour). Starch can be tapioca, corn, cassava, arrowroot, potato, or a combination of them. Note: Be aware when purchasing corn starch or potato starch, they should be clearly marked. On the other hand, corn flour and potato flour, which are not a starch, have fiber, protein, and flavor.

#2: Keep the "flour" or as I call it the "protein flour" component of the recipe to ⅔ of the total flour (i.e. 1 cup of starch with 2 cups of protein flour). There is much to learn about the various gluten-free flours on the market. I have noticed that some flours have an overpowering taste if too much is used in a recipe but may lend a very favorable taste in a smaller amount! One such example to me is quinoa flour. I adore it in bread and pizza crust recipes but at a smaller amount. Ironically, I enjoy eating the cooked grain often, but when milled and baked, it is a bit different. What one person likes or suggests may not be to your liking. As the kids got older, I wanted to add more nutrient-dense bread than our white bread, so I began to branch out. Here are some flours that you can use to make up the 2 cups or ⅔ of the total flour: quinoa flour, brown rice flour, teff flour, millet flour, amaranth flour, oat flour (certified gluten-free), tiger nut flour, sorghum flour, buckwheat flour, chickpea flour, corn flour, coconut flour, almond flour. *A good rule of thumb:* Add ½ tsp of gum (xanthan gum or guar gum) per cup of flour.

#3: Adding fiber is fantastic! You can add a Tbsp or so without having to adjust any flour measurements, but if you decide to add high-fiber flour, ground flax seeds, or flax meal, then you will count that as part of your ⅔ portion of the "protein flour." I try to keep the flax meal to no more than ⅓ cup, so the loaf isn't too heavy and the consistency is still smooth. Some companies make a gluten-free fiber you can add to your baking. I also like to add fine psyllium husk powder to my baking; it brings fantastic fiber and bounce to the bread!

#4: Water content. For a decade, I used the same recipe for the white bread I made for the kids' lunches. I stuck to 1 ½ cups of water, and they loved it. Yet, as I began playing around with the bread, I began to see that the water content could be tweaked depending on the flour I used. I reduced the water to 1 ¼ cup and it was different, but I liked it very much. I noticed some fiber-rich loaves need a touch more water. These are all things you will see for yourself as you begin playing with your recipes. Try not to get discouraged if you're experimenting. If a loaf comes out too stodgy, make toast or croutons — as long as the taste is good, there is hope! You will adjust next time!

#5: Play with oil. Sometimes I feel like having a loaf of bread using my special high-quality olive oil with a nutty rich flavor or a more neutral flavor found in the avocado oil. I stick only to using olive oil and avocado oil, but many people use vegetable oil and coconut oil.

Starters & Sides

Eggplant Genovese
Bacon Wrapped Shrimp
Corned Beef Dip
Garlic Almond Green Beans
Chicken Lettuce Wraps
Pickle Pasta
Potato Pancakes
Quick Garlic Aioli
Spinach Balls
QT Bake
Sesame Peas
Quick and Easy Avocado Drizzle
Our Special Guacamole
Peppers & Onions
Fajita Onions

Eggplant Genovese

Do you love fresh basil? How about eggplant? If you are a fan of both of those then you are going to LOVE this side dish. It melts in your mouth. It is often served as a side dish or vegetable of the meal, but if you fall in love with it like I have, you may make more and serve it as a meal.

PREP TIME: *10 minutes*   **COOK TIME:** *1 hour*   **OVEN TEMP:** *350°*   **TOOLS:** *8x8 inch baking dish*

INGREDIENTS

45 fresh basil leaves (1 ½- 2 cups)
½ cup grated parmesan cheese
3 cups Our Family's Tomato
   Sauce (page 139)
Olive oil spray

DIRECTIONS

1. Peel skin off of the eggplant with vegetable peeler and cut the ends off.

2. Slice the eggplant into ¼ inch disks.

3. Place on a baking sheet in a single layer, no overlapping. Spray with olive oil. Bake eggplant slices at 350° for 15 minutes.

4. With tongs, flip the eggplant over, spray again with oil, and bake for another 15 minutes.

5. Generously coat the bottom of the baking dish with your sauce.

6. Layer eggplant on top of the sauce.

7. Generously place basil over the eggplant. I like to place a piece of basil on top of each slice of eggplant, so that every bite gets a piece of basil.

8. Sprinkle cheese on top.

9. Repeat the layers: sauce, eggplant, basil, cheese. I like to end with an extra sprinkle of cheese on top.

10. Raise the oven temperature to 375° then bake for 30 minutes!

TWEAKS

_____

_____

_____

_____

_____

_____

_____

_____

_____

_____

Bacon-Wrapped Shrimp

Normally, I would recommend an appetizer like this one to be served on a warming tray, piping hot. But since I have been making this recipe, I have never seen it last more than four minutes. It's a huge hit!

PREP TIME: 30 minutes   **COOK TIME: 35-45 minutes**   **OVEN TEMP: 375°**

INGREDIENTS

1 pound raw shrimp
1 pound uncooked bacon
15-ounce can whole water
   chestnuts
1 ½ Tbsp chili garlic sauce

½ cup brown sugar
¼ cup ketchup
½ cup mayonnaise
1 tsp paprika
1 tsp garlic powder

DIRECTIONS

1. Devein and remove tail from shrimp (if this is already done for you your prep time will be reduced). Set aside.
2. In a medium mixing bowl, mix together chili garlic sauce, brown sugar, ketchup, mayonnaise, paprika, and garlic powder. Set aside.
3. Cut bacon in half.
4. Wrap a piece of shrimp with a piece of bacon. Secure with a toothpick.
5. Lay the shrimp on the lined baking sheet.
6. Repeat until all the shrimp are wrapped.
7. Place the water chestnuts on the baking sheet.
8. Pour the spice mixture on top of the shrimp and water chestnuts.
9. Place in the oven to bake for 25-35 minutes. To make them extra crispy, broil for 1-2 minutes and keep a close eye.

TIPS

- If you have run out of bacon and you have extra shrimp, place them on the baking sheet as well and cover in this delicious sauce. You will not be disappointed — that sauce would taste great on a shoe!

- If you have extra bacon and a little extra time, wrap those water chestnuts too!

- Use a spatula to spread the sauce on the shrimp evenly.

TWEAKS

_____

_____

_____

Corned Beef Dip

PREP TIME: 10-15 minutes   *BAKE TIME: 30 minutes*   *OVEN TEMP: 350°*   *TOOLS: 8x8 inch baking dish*

INGREDIENTS

8 ounces cooked corned beef
8 ounces cream cheese
5 ounces Greek yogurt (can use low fat if you prefer)

4 ounces Swiss cheese
10-ounce can sauerkraut (NOT Bavarian style)
2 cloves garlic, minced

DIRECTIONS

1. Chop corned beef into small pieces, until almost shredded.
2. Chop Swiss cheese (if not shredded already) into small cubes.
3. Into a medium-sized bowl, add beef, cheese, and all the remaining ingredients.
4. Mix well.
5. Place in a baking dish and cook for 30 minutes until golden brown and bubbling.

TIPS

- Serve with toasted gluten-free rye bread or sourdough, or rice/seed/multi-grain crackers.

Garlic Almond Green Beans

A consistent family favorite. We don't just wait until the holidays, we make it year-round because it is so easy and delicious!

PREP TIME: *5 minutes*   **COOK TIME:** *9-10 minutes*   **TOOLS:** *3-quart saucepan*

INGREDIENTS

2 Tbsp extra virgin olive oil
12 ounces organic green beans
2 Tbsp dried garlic slices (see Tips)

⅓ cup sliced almonds
½ tsp garlic powder
¼ tsp salt

DIRECTIONS

1. Clean green beans and trim the ends.
2. Preheat a saucepan on high with 1 Tbsp of oil.
3. Place fresh green beans in the pan and move them around for 4-5 minutes, drizzle the remaining 1 Tbsp of oil.
4. Add dried garlic and garlic powder, mix and move around in the pan.
5. Add the sliced almonds and stir them around.
6. Add the salt, stir again. Cook an additional 3-4 minutes stirring the whole time so that nothing burns.
7. Ready to serve nice and hot and crunchy!

TIPS

- If you can't find dried sliced garlic, or if you and your family don't care for a strong garlic dish, you can use the dried minced garlic or garlic powder. If you are only using the garlic powder I suggest increasing to 1 ½-2 tsp.

TWEAKS

_____
_____
_____
_____
_____
_____
_____

Chicken Lettuce Wraps

PREP TIME: 25 minutes   *TOTAL TIME: 25 minutes*

INGREDIENTS

Dip/Drizzle Sauce:
¼ cup cane sugar
½ cup water
2 Tbsp liquid aminos
2 Tbsp rice vinegar
1 Tbsp chili garlic sauce
1 Tbsp potato starch
½ tsp sesame oil
½ Tbsp lemon juice
1 Tbsp cooking sherry

Veggies:
3 Tbsp avocado oil
3 cloves garlic
7-8 scallions (large)
1 ½-2 tsp grated ginger
12 ounces white mushrooms, cubed
5-ounce can water chestnuts, diced
½ Tbsp cooking sherry
1 Tbsp Tamari
½ tsp sesame oil
½ Tbsp hoisin sauce
1 Tbsp cane sugar

Meat:
1 pound ground organic chicken
1 Tbsp cooking sherry
1 Tbsp lemon juice
¼ cup water
1 Tbsp Tamari
2 tsp chili garlic sauce
½ Tbsp hoisin sauce
1 Tbsp potato starch
1 head romaine lettuce leaves, cleaned

DIRECTIONS

Sauce:
1. Mix together all ingredients and place in a medium frying pan.
2. Over medium heat, warm the sauce, whisking periodically. At the same time, start making vegetables.

For Vegtables:
3. Into a large saucepan, add avocado oil, scallions, and garlic and begin to sauté.
4. After 3 minutes, add mushrooms and water chestnuts and continue to cook for 3-4 minutes.
5. Add cooking sherry, tamari, sesame oil, hoisin sauce, and sugar and cook for 3 more minutes.
6. Take the vegetables off the heat, place in a bowl, and set aside.

Meat:
7. Place the ground chicken into the same saucepan as the veggies (that still has remnants of sauce from veggies) and brown the meat. While it is cooking, take a spatula and break the meat up into tiny pieces.
8. Add cooking sherry, lemon juice, water, Tamari, chili garlic sauce, hoisin sauce and cook for 3 minutes.

TIPS

Take this dish from side to the main show:

- Double the recipe and serve with a side of Vermicelli Rice Noodles (Angel Hair) with some of this delicious sauce or sweet chili sauce! Serve with a side of steamed broccoli!

- This dish can also be made into a salad! Place cut Romaine lettuce in a bowl with a serving of rice noodles, top with this delicious chicken and drizzle with sauce!

- If you don't have garlic chili sauce then you can use sriracha as it has similar flavors.

9. Add potato starch and mix into the meat.
10. Add the veggies and mix well.
11. Serve with romaine lettuce. Place some of the mixture onto the lettuce and drizzle the sauce on top!

TWEAKS

_____

_____

_____

_____

_____

Pickle Pasta

With its salty, tangy flavor and the smoothness of the dressing, this pickle pasta dish has been named, "The Best Flipping Pasta Salad Ever" by my family. When my kids were younger, I had to break the news to them that I couldn't make it two times a week.

PREP TIME: 5 minutes   **COOK TIME:** 8-10 minutes

INGREDIENTS

1 pound elbow rice pasta, cooked according to directions
6 whole dill pickles, diced
¼ cup red wine vinegar

½ tsp fine garlic powder
½ tsp fine onion powder
½ cup mayonnaise
Salt, to taste

DIRECTIONS

1. Cook pasta according to directions on the package, strain, cool a bit with cold water for 30 seconds-1 minute. Drain well then place in a large mixing bowl.
2. Cut pickles and add to the bowl.
3. Add mayonnaise, vinegar, onion powder, and garlic powder.
4. Mix well and serve!

TIPS

- The pickle is a perfect amount of salt for most people so I don't have any in the ingredients, but you may like a dash more. I suggest you start with a little dash at a time until you find your perfect level of salt.

- GF pasta cold can be tricky as a leftover. If the pasta is cooked long enough and has soaked up the seasonings it may just need to hit room temperature to be eaten out of the fridge. Sometimes I drizzle a tiny bit of water over it and place it in the microwave for 15 seconds at a time. The goal is not to get it hot but to "reconstitute" the pasta.

- I prefer the pasta in this recipe to be cooked until soft and not al denté.

TWEAKS

_____
_____
_____
_____
_____
_____

Pickle Pasta (pictured above).

Potato Pancakes

Need a quick side that can complement just about any meal? Look no further!
Step these potato pancakes up a notch with a side of garlic aioli and pimentos.

PREP TIME: 5 minutes   **TOTAL TIME:** 14-16 minutes   **OVEN TEMP:** 400°

INGREDIENTS

1 russet potato
1 tsp dried minced onion
½ tsp onion powder
¼ tsp salt
1 tsp potato starch
1 Tbsp rice flour
1 egg, beaten
2-3 Tbsp avocado oil

DIRECTIONS

1. Peel and grate the potato.

2. Mix together all the ingredients.

3. Allow to sit for 5-10 minutes.

4. Add avocado oil to a frying pan.

5. Using a measuring cup, scoop ¼ cup of the mixture and add to the frying pan. Flatten slightly with the bottom of the cup.

6. Quickly brown the pancake on each side, about 2 minutes per side.

7. Place finished pancakes on a parchment-lined tray and put in the air fryer for 10-12 minutes. Crunchy perfection!

TIPS

• If you have an air fryer or convection setting, I would suggest you use that for an evenly crunchy pancake.

TWEAKS

_____

_____

_____

Quick Garlic Aioli

PREP TIME: 10 minutes   COOK TIME: 10 minutes   OVEN TEMP: 400°

INGREDIENTS

10-12 garlic cloves
2 Tbsp extra virgin olive oil
½ cup mayonnaise
1 Tbsp fresh lemon juice
½ tsp sea salt
½ tsp pepper

TWEAKS

_____

_____

_____

_____

_____

_____

_____

_____

_____

DIRECTIONS

1. **Roast the garlic:** Take your garlic cloves. Cut the tip of each off. Cover in olive oil and salt and place in tin foil. Make it like a little pouch or bundle and leave a small hole to allow steam to vent out. Roast garlic in the oven for 20 minutes at 400°. Or try your hand at roasting the garlic in a frying pan. Just make sure your garlic is peeled and does NOT burn. Move the garlic around often to avoid burning. Should be slightly golden brown after around 6-8 minutes.

2. Allow the garlic to cool down.

3. Add the garlic and to a small food processor and blitz until smooth. (Can use the oil from the frying pan if you like.)

4. Add all the rest of the ingredients to the food processor and blend until very smooth.

TIPS

- You can absolutely use a toaster oven or an air fryer to roast the garlic. Coat the garlic in oil then place it the same as mentioned above.

- If you choose to remove the skin of the garlic, check the garlic around the 10-minute mark. They tend to go much faster without the skin and begin to brown. The softer roasted garlic is slightly better for making a quick aioli though.

- Roasted garlic makes a _tasty_ treat when they are a tad crunchy with a touch of salt.

Spinach Balls

PREP TIME: 20 minutes   *COOK TIME: 18-22 minutes*

INGREDIENTS

10-ounce box frozen chopped
  spinach
3 eggs, beaten
1 Tbsp extra virgin olive oil
1 cup shredded sharp cheddar
  cheese
⅔ cup gluten-free breadcrumbs

¼ tsp salt
½ tsp pepper
1 tsp dried parsley
¼ - ½ tsp garlic powder
6 shakes Tabasco sauce (6 shakes
  more if you like it hotter!)

DIRECTIONS

1. Place the spinach box in the microwave for 2-3 minutes until defrosted. Set aside to cool.

2. In a large bowl mix together the cheese, bread crumbs, salt, pepper, parsley, garlic powder.

3. Squeeze excess water out of the spinach. Place the spinach into the cheese mixture. Mix.

4. Add oil, eggs, and Tabasco sauce.

5. Form into balls and place on a parchment-lined baking sheet.

6. Bake at 375° for 18-22 minutes.

7. Serve with Quick Garlic Aioli (page 39).

TIPS

- I like to use the convection oven or air fryer with this recipe. I start taking a look in the oven around 18 minutes. If I see the cheese begin to bubble and become golden then I know it's time!

- Wet hands help. I do about 5 and wet my hands and carry on.

- I have a range for garlic powder because you may choose not to serve these spinach balls with garlic aioli and you want that ball to have all the garlic goodness.

- I have made this recipe fresh spinach but I prefer to make it with frozen spinach. If you can't find frozen chopped spinach, here is a method for fresh spinach: Loosely chop the spinach and place in a frying pan with ½ Tbsp olive oil or avocado oil. Stir constantly with a spoon until completely wilted. You can add ½ Tbsp of water to speed the process up, but it should only take 2-3 minutes in total. Allow cool before continuing on with the recipe.

TWEAKS

_____

_____

_____

_____

QT Bake

PREP TIME: 25 minutes   *BAKE TIME: 30 minutes*   *OVEN TEMP: 375°*   *TOOLS: 9x9 inch baking dish*

INGREDIENTS

- 2 cups cooked Teff (about 1 cup dry; cook according to package directions)
- 2 cups cooked Quinoa (about 1 cup dry; cook according to package directions)
- 4 pieces cooked bacon, crisp
- 1 cup onion, diced
- 2 large scallions, chopped (½ cup)
- 2 celery stalks, diced (½ cup)
- 2 Tbsp extra virgin olive oil
- ¾ tsp salt
- ½ tsp pepper
- ½ tsp fine garlic powder
- ½ tsp Italian seasoning
- 1 large egg
- 4 egg whites
- ½ cup sour cream
- 1 cup mozzarella, shredded

DIRECTIONS

1. Cook teff and quinoa. Set aside.
2. Sauté vegetables and season with salt, pepper, garlic powder, and Italian seasoning.
3. Mix vegetables, quinoa, teff, egg, egg whites, and sour cream.
4. Place in a baking dish and top with mozzarella.
5. Bake at 375°F for 30 minutes.
6. Cut and serve!

TIPS

- Need to be dairy free? Try using the cashew cheese found in the Vegetable Lasagna (page 120) to replace the sourcream and the mozzarella on top.
- If you use a larger baking dish, reduce the cook time by 5 minutes so that your bake doesn't dry out too much.

TWEAKS

_____

_____

Sesame Peas

PREP TIME: 1 minute   *COOK TIME: 4 minutes*

INGREDIENTS

½ pound of peas, either sugar
   snap peas or snow peas
½-1 Tbsp avocado oil
1 tsp sesame oil

¼ tsp Himalayan salt
½ Tbsp real maple syrup
1 Tbsp roasted sesame seeds

DIRECTIONS

1. Add avocado oil to a large frying pan and allow it to warm up over medium heat.

2. Place the peas into the oil and stir constantly for 2 minutes.

3. Sprinkle the salt and maple syrup on the peas and stir for less than a minute.

4. Remove from the stove top and sprinkle the sesame oil and seeds on top.

TWEAKS

_____

_____

_____

_____

_____

Quick and Easy Avocado Drizzle

PREP TIME: 5 minutes

INGREDIENTS

- ½ cup local honey
- ½ tsp dried parsley
- ¾ tsp garlic powder
- 1 Tbsp soy sauce (or tamari or liquid aminos)

DIRECTIONS

1. Mix well and drizzle over avocado slices.
2. Enough for 4 avocados.

TIPS

- To prevent browning of unused avocado either store (in refrigerator) with the pit in the container or sprinkle with lemon juice.

Our Special Guacamole

PREP TIME: 15-20 minutes

INGREDIENTS

3 ripe avocadoes, diced
2 small garlic cloves, pressed
1 cup fresh cilantro, chopped
½ large onion, diced small (about 1 cup)

2 medium tomatoes (about 1 ½ cups diced)
3 TBS fresh lime juice (2 limes)
1 tsp Himalayan salt
½ tsp pepper

DIRECTIONS

1. Mince garlic fine or use garlic press. Add to a medium mixing bowl.
2. Dice the onion and tomatoes. (Cut the tomatoes in half and remove the seeds, then dice.) Add to the bowl.
3. Loosely chop the cilantro. Add to the bowl.
4. Cut avocado into pieces. It's fine if the pieces are different sizes or some of the avocado has to be scraped out of the skin. Just make sure it ALL makes it into the bowl!
5. Squeeze the limes into the bowl.
6. Mix well.
7. Add salt and pepper and mix again.
8. Cover and place in the refrigerator for at least 30 minutes for the best taste!

TWEAKS

_____

_____

_____

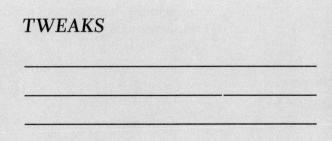

Peppers & Onions

PREP TIME: 5 minutes   COOK TIME: 8-10 minutes

DIRECTIONS

1. Peel the onion then cut it in half. Slice thin.
2. Cut the green pepper in half, remove seeds, and cut into strips.
3. Preheat a cast iron skillet over a medium flame. Add avocado oil to the skillet.
4. Add onions and peppers to the skillet and stir around to avoid burning.
5. As onions and peppers begin to cook add garlic powder, salt, and pepper.
6. When the onions look caramelized and the peppers are slightly brown in spots and look cooked but yet still firm (if they're mushy they've cooked too much), then remove from the stove and serve.

INGREDIENTS

1 large onion, sliced
2 green bell peppers, sliced
1 Tbsp avocado oil
2 tsp garlic powder
½ tsp salt
½ tsp black pepper

Fajita Onions

PREP TIME: 5 minutes   COOK TIME: 6-8 minutes

DIRECTIONS

1. Peel onion then cut in half. Slice thin.
2. Preheat a cast iron skillet over a high flame. Add avocado oil to the skillet.
3. Add onions to the skillet and stir around to avoid burning.
4. As onions begin to caramelize add fresh cilantro, stir.
5. Add fajita seasoning and stir until all the onions are coated nicely.
6. After about 2-3 minutes, add lemon juice. Stir for an additional 30 seconds-1 minute. Remove from stove and serve.

INGREDIENTS

1 medium onion, sliced
½ Tbsp avocado oil
1 Tbsp Jen's Fajita seasoning (page 107)
1 Tbsp lemon juice
¼ cup fresh cilantro

Soups and Salads

Split Pea Soup
Stew Time
Lentil Soup
Chicken Broth/Stock/Bone Broth
My Favorite Veggie Soup
Colorful Quinoa Salad
Basic Go-To Dressing
Beet Salad
Epic Caesar Dressing
Old Faithful Cucumber Salad
Twist on Tabbouleh
Kale and Brussels Sprouts Salad
Kale Salad and So Much More
Ginger Dressing

Split Pea Soup

We love this soup paired with Focaccia Bread (page 92). It's hearty enough to be a meal!

PREP TIME: *10 minutes*   COOK TIME: *1 hour +*   TOOLS: *Stock pot*

INGREDIENTS

2 ½-3 Tbsp extra virgin olive oil
1 large onion, diced (about 1 cup)
1 large (or 2 medium) carrot, peeled and diced

2 celery stalks, diced
⅓ pound smoked ham, cubed
16-ounce bag dried green split peas

3-4 cups water
3-4 cups chicken broth

DIRECTIONS

1. Rinse peas in a strainer, looking through peas to make sure there isn't anything other than peas in there.

2. In a large sauce pot add: olive oil, onions, celery, carrots and ham.

3. Sauté for about 6 minutes or until the veggies are soft.

4. Add peas, water, and chicken broth to the pot. Liquid should cover everything and also be at least 2-3 inches from the top for room.

5. Cover and bring to a boil. Then reduce heat to a simmer for 1 hour. Stir occasionally.

6. After an hour, check if the consistency is to your preference.

7. **If you like a thinner soup:** Either add additional liquid (broth or water) or begin eating!

8. **If you prefer a thicker soup:** Remove the top and cook for an additional 10-15 minutes.

TIPS

• In a pinch I have used deli ham and even bacon.

• Can use homemade Chicken Broth (page 57) or store-bought. If you have a craving for this soup and don't have any chicken broth on hand, use water! You can play around with seasoning. In past soups I have used 1 tsp of poultry seasoning, garlic powder, or onion powder when using water to give it a chicken flavor; or you can let the veggies stand on their own!

• If you don't want to add meat to this soup, add ½ tsp salt.

TWEAKS

_____
_____
_____
_____
_____
_____
_____
_____
_____
_____
_____
_____
_____

Stew Time

My husband grew up loving beef stew. My mother-in-law was a pro at making stew and big meats (roasts, etc.). I had a lot to be compared to but I was up for the challenge! My gluten-eater, lover of Mom's stew, was going to be "Lover of MY Gluten-Free Stew" if it was the last thing I did. Challenge accepted (and won)!

PREP TIME: *20 minutes*   **COOK TIME:** *2-8 hours*   **TOOLS:** *8 quart Crock-Pot*

INGREDIENTS

2 pounds stew meat, cubed (beef)

1 cup gluten-free all-purpose flour

½ tsp salt

½ tsp black pepper

½ tsp onion powder

½ tsp garlic powder

½ tsp dried parsley

6 celery stalks, cut into ½ inch pieces

5 carrots, cut into ½ inch pieces

1 ½ onion, cut into ½ inch pieces

3 Tbsp avocado oil, divided

32 ounces beef broth

2 potatoes, peeled and cubed

1-2 cups water

1 Tbsp butter

DIRECTIONS

1. In a medium-sized frying pan, add 2 Tbsp oil and heat on medium-high.

2. In a medium-sized mixing bowl add gluten-free flour, salt, pepper, onion powder, garlic powder, and parsley. Mix well.

3. Add several pieces of beef to the flour mixture, cover the meat completely.

4. Shake the excess flour from the meat and place a few pieces in the frying pan at a time, leaving space to flip and the pieces. This step is not intended to fully cook the meat — just to brown it. When browned, transfer to a crock pot or large pot.

5. Continue with remaining beef until all the meat is browned and placed in pot.

6. Add celery, onion, and carrots to the pot. (Reserve ¼ of the vegetables to add in at the end if you want a crunchier stew bite, during step 11.)

7. Pour in the beef broth. Reserve ½ cup of the broth for a roux.

8. Make a roux with some of the remaining flour. Into a saucepan, add 1 Tbsp oil and 1 Tbsp butter. Melt, then slowly add ½ cup of the reserved flour while stirring and ½ cup broth. When thick, add to the pot. If a little clumpy, no worries.

9. Stir everything very well in the pot.

10. Allow to cook for 8 hours on "low" setting of the Crock-Pot (or 2 hours on medium on the stove) I still stir the stew in the crock pot at least 2-3 times. On the stove you need to watch more carefully to avoid burning.

11. Add potatoes and any optional reserved vegetables about 30-45

minutes before the stew is done cooking.

12. Optional: Serve with wild rice, cooked to package directions.

TIPS

- Stew Challenge! Often my hubby requests stew that is lower in carbs. I make it exactly as I shared with you but omit the potatoes, bread bowl (sad face), and I make the roux just a bit less thick. I might add a side of wild rice (rich in fiber) for the bottom of the bowl. Delish.

- If you want a thicker stew, add more of your the seasoned flour you used for the roux.

- You can use rice flour if you don't have gluten-free all-purpose flour.

TWEAKS

_____

_____

_____

_____

_____

_____

_____

_____

Lentil Soup

PREP TIME: *15 minutes*   **COOK TIME:** *1-2 hours*   **TOOLS:** *Stock pot*

INGREDIENTS

16-ounce bag dried lentils
4-5 cups chicken broth (or water
   or a combination of both)
1 ½-2 Tbsp extra virgin olive oil
1 carrot, diced

3 celery stalks, diced
1 medium sweet onion, diced
1 tsp garlic powder
½ tsp salt
½ tsp pepper

DIRECTIONS

1. Rinse the lentils in a strainer first, removing anything that is not a lentil!
2. In a pot, add the oil and sauté the vegetables. Cook until soft.
3. Add the lentils and chicken broth (or water). Make sure to cover veggies and lentils with the liquid. Leave room at the top of the pot to ensure the soup doesn't boil over.
4. Season with some salt, pepper, and garlic powder.
5. Bring to a boil then lower the stove temperature to a simmer. Simmer for 1 hour.
6. At the halfway point, uncover and stir. If you see that the soup needs more liquid, add at this time.

TIPS

- I allow my cook time to be more toward the 1 ½- 2 hour mark to achieve a softer lentil; it's just my preference. And OH BOY does it taste good with pasta. If you get a softer lentil and add pasta to it, it forms like a lentil paste over the pasta. This lentil pasta option brings back so many childhood memories on how my mom used to make lentil pasta.
- Lentils are high in protein and fiber. They have a good amount of iron, potassium, and calcium. Potassium, folate, and iron found in lentils have amazing benefits.

TWEAKS

_____
_____
_____
_____
_____
_____
_____
_____
_____
_____
_____
_____
_____

Chicken Broth/Stock/Bone Broth

PREP TIME: 20 minutes   *COOK TIME: 1-12 hours*   *TOOLS: Crock-Pot*

INGREDIENTS

1 large onion, cut into big chinks
4 cloves garlic, peeled and whole
4 celery stalks, cut into large chunks

3 carrots, peeled and cut into large chunks
1 chicken carcass, skin and most of the meat removed (see Tips)

2 tsp salt
2 tsp pepper

DIRECTIONS

1. Place roast chicken carcass into your largest stock pot (see Roasted Chicken recipe page 123).
2. Add all ingredients to the pot and cover, leaving room at the top to keep the broth from boiling over.
3. Season with salt and black pepper.
4. Bring to a boil then lower to a simmer. Simmer for at least 1 hour. The longer it goes the more flavor it develops. I usually let it go for 5 hours or 10-12 hours to achieve bone broth status!
5. Through the cooking process, you may find that you need to go in and add a bit of water.
6. Once you are ready to use the broth, or ready to cool it down and store it, you will need to strain the large pieces and any smaller pieces, like tiny bones, that may be present and discard. Take a pair of tongs and remove as many large pieces as you can.
7. Take another large pot and place a strainer on top, then slowly pour the broth into the strainer and store.

TIPS

- I usually roast whole chickens and place the carcass in the freezer for this recipe.
- Cool that broth down before storing. The method I use: fill a large sealable bag with ice, place in broth, and allow to cool for about 1 hour before storing in the refrigerator.
- You can store in the freezer for up to 4 months.

USE THIS STOCK IN MANY WAYS:

- You can use the carcass of the chicken from your own Roasted Chicken! Turn to page 123 for the recipe!
- My Favorite Veggie Soup (page 58).
- Use this broth in pasta dishes or in place of water when boiling pasta for added flavor.
- Use in Lentil Soup (page 54) or Split Pea Soup (page 51).
- Freeze the broth in an ice cube tray to add to certain dishes for a splash of flavor.
- Bone Broth sipping: I enjoy sipping bone broth. I especially enjoy/need this intestinal break after weeks of holiday eating! This broth is higher in protein and nutrients, is good for intestinal/digestive health, and can even help with controlling cravings.

My Favorite Veggie Soup

FRESH VEGGIES PREP TIME: 15 minutes
FROZEN VEGGIES PREP TIME: 5 minutes

COOK TIME: 30 minutes-1 hour
COOK TIME: 20-30 minutes

INGREDIENTS

15-20 ounces broccoli florets, steamed
20 ounces cauliflower, steamed
3 Tbsp extra virgin olive oil
1 large sweet onion, diced

4 cloves garlic, minced
3 celery stalks, cut into ½ inch pieces
3 carrots, peeled and cut into ½ inch pieces

10 ounces kale
10 ounces spinach
Chicken Broth (page 57)

DIRECTIONS

1. Take your cut and cleaned broccoli and place in a microwaveable bowl with ½ cup water and steam for minutes). Repeat for cauliflower.

2. In a large pot over medium heat add olive oil then sauté onion, garlic, celery, and carrots until slightly cooked.

3. Add kale, broccoli, cauliflower, spinach, and broth.

4. Add salt and pepper.

5. Mix well.

6. Allow to come to a boil then lower heat to simmer for 30 minutes for crunchier vegetables. Simmer for an hour for softer veggies.

To Make My Favorite Veggie Soup With Frozen Vegetables:
Sauté onion, garlic, celery, and carrots until slightly cooked. Add broth, salt, and pepper. Then add in any combination of frozen vegetables (see Tips). Do not overcook when using frozen vegetables.

TIPS

- Frozen vegetable combination: broccoli florets (14 ounces), chopped spinach (10 ounces), and cauliflower rice (10 ounces).

- My freezer staples that make a great soup (use any combination): broccoli florets, broccoli chopped, cauliflower rice, spinach chopped, turnip greens, mustard greens, green peas, and lima beans!

- Benefits of frozen veggies: Reliable all year because they are grown then frozen when they are in season and they maintain their nutrients! So yes, fresh is great, when in season, and frozen is pretty darn awesome too!

- Serve with my Fast & Easy Rolls (page 89).

TWEAKS

_____

_____

_____

_____

Colorful Quinoa Salad

PREP TIME: 30 minutes   *COOK TIME: 20 minutes*

INGREDIENTS

4 cups tri-colored organic quinoa
½ red (or orange) pepper, diced
¼ medium red onion, diced
   (about ¼ cup)
2 cloves garlic, minced

1 avocado, diced
1 medium tomato, diced (about
   1 cup)
2 Tbsp lemon juice
3 Tbsp red wine vinegar

¼ cup extra virgin olive oil
½ tsp Himalayan salt
½ tsp black pepper

DIRECTIONS

1. Cook quinoa according to the package directions, fluff with a fork when done and allow to cool.

2. Cut pepper, onion, garlic, avocado, and tomato.

3. Add all the ingredients into a large bowl. Mix well.

4. Cover and place in the refrigerator, to allow to marinate for at least 1 hour for the best taste.

TWEAKS

_____

_____

_____

_____

_____

Basic Go-To Dressing

PREP TIME: 8 minutes

INGREDIENTS

- ⅓ cup + 2 Tbsp extra virgin olive oil
- ⅓ cup red wine vinegar
- 1 Tbsp balsamic vinegar
- 2 small cloves garlic, pressed in garlic press
- 2 Tbsp (2 slices) sweet onion, pressed in garlic press
- ½ tsp Himalayan salt
- ½ tsp black pepper
- ½ tsp dried Italian seasoning

DIRECTIONS

1. Using a garlic press, press the garlic and onion and place into a dressing shaker.
2. Measure all the ingredients out and add to the shaker.
3. Shake really well and do so each time you use.

TIPS

- Add ½-1 Tbsp sugar to change it up.
- Add a few dashes of Tabasco sauce for some heat.
- Store in refrigerator.

TWEAKS

_____
_____
_____
_____
_____
_____
_____
_____
_____

Beet Salad

PREP TIME: 5 minutes   *COOK TIME: 30 '0 minutes*

INGREDIENTS

3 beets (about 10 ounces)
½ sweet onion, sliced thin
2 tsp extra virgin olive oil

2 Tbsp red wine vinegar
½ tsp salt
⅛ tsp pepper

DIRECTIONS

1. Cut the greens off the beet. Peel the beets, then cut into quarters.
2. Place beets into a pot of water. Boil or steam beets.

   Steam: Cut the beet into quarters. For a large beet, cut the beet in half and then into thirds. Place into a steaming basket and into a sauce pot. Add water to the bottom, place beets in the basket and steam for 25-30 minutes, until a fork can easily go through.

   Boiling: Boil for 20-30 minutes, until a fork can easily go through. Cool in cold water.
3. Using a mandolin slicer, slice the onion. If you don't have one, cut as thin as you can get them with a knife. Place in a bowl.
4. Once cool, (carefully) using the guard, slice the beet on the mandolin slicer, add to the bowl.
5. Add olive oil, vinegar, salt, and pepper.

TIPS

- If you aren't lucky enough to have a farmers' market near you, you can find beets (usually with the greens) in a bundle of 3. I based this recipe on that.
- DO NOT throw away the beet greens! Cut them from the beet, clean and chop them and sauté them with onions in olive oil and enjoy. The greens are so delicious!
- This recipe is fantastic served with goat cheese or feta!
- Beets are a nutritious root vegetable packed with potassium, nitrates, and antioxidants. One cup of raw beet has 2.2 grams of protein, 3.8 g of fiber, and 13g of carbohydrates.
- Growing up, my family made this recipe by boiling the beets which lessens the strong taste of beets BUT also loses some of the color which is where your phytonutrients can be found. I suggest steaming or roasting the beets to get all you can from this lovely root veggie!

TWEAKS

_____
_____
_____
_____
_____
_____

Epic Caesar Dressing

This recipe has no raw or pasteurized eggs or mustard. But being a true lover of Caesar salad, I came up with this recipe years ago because I've never been a fan of mustard so I wanted a recipe that was delicious without it. I like this recipe for its simplicity and the lack of searching for pasteurized eggs or pasteurizing them myself. I hope you enjoy this as much as we do.

PREP TIME: 10 minutes

INGREDIENTS

- 1 clove garlic
- 2 lemons, juiced (about ¼ cup juice)
- 1 tsp Worcestershire sauce
- 1 Tbsp anchovy paste (or 4-5 anchovy filets)
- Salt and pepper, to taste
- 1 ounce grated parmesan cheese (fresh)
- ¼ cup extra virgin olive oil

DIRECTIONS

1. In a food processor add garlic, lemon juice, Worcestershire sauce, anchovies, salt, pepper, and parmesan cheese.
2. Add the olive oil to the food processor very slowly while mixing. After about 2-3 minutes, the dressing will turn creamy.
3. Keep refrigerated.

TWEAKS

_____

_____

TIPS

- **Dairy-Free Version:** This is where the addition of salt will be necessary and not optional as I have above. Add 1 tsp of salt. I've made this recipe dairy free for our oldest daughter and it was a BIG hit!

- I use a small, easy to clean, 3.5 cup food processor for these quick recipes. I go for the easiest way to make a recipe so I can move on to the next dish!

Old Faithful Cucumber Salad

I can always rely on this simple and refreshing salad to bring a smile to the faces around my table.

PREP TIME: 10 minutes

INGREDIENTS

2 medium cucumbers, sliced
½ medium sweet onion, sliced
1-2 tsp cane sugar

2 Tbsp white wine vinegar
½ Tbsp dried dill
2 Tbsp mayonnaise (or olive oil)

½ tsp salt
Optional: 1 medium tomato, diced

DIRECTIONS

1. Scrub the cucumbers clean with a vegetable brush.
2. Cut the ends of the cucumbers off. Using a peeler, take a strip of the skin off, then leave a strip on and repeat that pattern to give a pretty green color to the salad.
3. Using a mandolin slicer, slice the cucumbers and onion.
4. Add all ingredients to a large bowl and mix well.
5. You can serve this salad as is or add in the optional tomato. Cut tomato into quarters and remove the flesh and seeds, then dice. Add to salad, mix and serve!

TIPS

- BE CAREFUL with that mandolin slicer. I always feel like I need to say that whenever I suggest someone using one. No kitchen accidents on my watch. Always use the guard and watch your fingertips!

Twist on Tabbouleh

I love this version of tabbouleh (tabouli) with either cooked quinoa or buckwheat. I remember it so fondly from my gluten years and I found a way to enjoy it gluten-free! Believe me when I say, I often make BOTH because this salad is a big hit for anyone that has ever tried it.

PREP TIME: 25 minutes   *COOK TIME: 15-20 minutes*

INGREDIENTS

- 4 cups cooked buckwheat (or quinoa)
- 4 cups fresh Italian parsley (about 2 cups finely chopped)
- 3 medium tomatoes, diced
- 1 large sweet onion, diced (about 1 ½ cup)
- 3 cloves garlic, pressed or minced
- 3 lemons, juiced (about ⅓ cup + 1 Tbsp juice)
- ¼ cup extra virgin olive oil
- ½ Tbsp Himalayan salt

DIRECTIONS

1. Cook the grain. Set aside to cool completely.
2. Soak the parsley and rinse well. Remove large stems and dry well then chop finely. Add to large mixing bowl.
3. Cut tomatoes in half and remove the seeds from the middle. Then dice them and place in the bowl.
4. Cut onions, press garlic in the garlic press, and add to the bowl.
5. Add in lemon juice, olive oil, and salt.
6. Add the cooked grain and mix well.
7. Chill for at least an hour before serving.

TIPS

- Cook grain according to package directions. Usually 4 cups of cooked grain is a ratio of 1 cup dry buckwheat or quinoa and 2 cups of water.
- The buckwheat recipe can handle MORE parsley because of the size of the grain. Your taste buds will like the addition of ½ cup more parsley!
- Change it up: Add 1 medium cucumber, diced.

HEALTH BENEFITS

- Buckwheat helps regulate blood sugar, is high in magnesium, potassium and calcium, can help lower blood pressure, and its higher fiber content helps improve cholesterol which helps with heart health.

- Quinoa is rich in antioxidants and helps with lowering cholesterol and blood sugar.

- Parsley contains a variety of antioxidants (like flavonoids, carotenoids, and Vitamin C) which not only help in the prevention of cancer but help to soothe inflammation. Parsley also contains lutein, zeaxanthin, and beta carotene (plant compounds that protect eye health), is high in Vitamin K, and supports bone health.

Kale and Brussels Sprouts Salad

PREP TIME: 25 minutes

INGREDIENTS

1 pound organic kale
10 ounces brussel sprouts (about 14 sprouts), thinly sliced
½ sweet onion, thinly sliced
2 avocados, diced

1 medium cucumber, diced
2 lemons, juiced (about 3-4 Tbsp juice)
2 Tbsp apple cider vinegar
3 Tbsp avocado oil

1 tsp salt
2 Tbsp nutritional yeast
½ Tbsp fine garlic powder

DIRECTIONS

1. Remove stems from the kale and chop large pieces into bite-sized pieces. Place in a large mixing bowl.
2. Using a mandolin slicer, thinly slice the onion and brussels sprouts. If you don't have one, cut as thin as you can get them with a knife. Place in a bowl.
3. Dice the avocado and cucumber. Set aside.
4. Add lemon juice, apple cider vinegar, avocado oil, salt, nutritional yeast, and garlic powder to the kale bowl.
5. Mix really well. With gloved hands you can work the kale, squeezing and massaging the leaves, while also mixing ingredients around. By doing this, you are breaking down the kale so that it is easier to eat and better at soaking up all the flavors.
6. Next, add the avocados and cucumbers and mix once again until evenly distributed.
7. For the best tasting salad allow it to chill.

TIPS

- I often peel my cucumber by peeling every other line. Sometimes my family members don't care for the skin of the cucumber so I began doing this so we could still get a little skin for that fiber and color pop.
- *Slivered brussels sprouts:* Hold the stem and use the mandolin slicer slowly. You will have a small piece of the sprout left, simply use your knife and cut the remaining piece.

TWEAKS

_____

_____

_____

Kale Salad and So Much More

PREP TIME: 20 minutes

INGREDIENTS

15 ounces organic kale
1 large lemon, juiced (about 1 Tbsp juice)
2 Tbsp extra virgin olive oil
2 Tbsp apple cider vinegar

1 medium sweet onion, diced (about 1 cup)
1 avocado, diced
1 cup (8 ounces) canned chickpeas, drained

1 large tomato, diced
½ tsp Himalayan salt
½ tsp black pepper
1 tsp fine garlic powder
¼ cup nutritional yeast

DIRECTIONS

1. Remove the stems on the kale and cut into smaller bite-sized pieces and place into a large mixing bowl.

2. Pour olive oil, vinegar, and lemon juice on top.

3. Massage the kale with the liquid ingredients. This will help the vegetables to absorb all the yumminess!

4. Sprinkle the onion, avocado, chickpeas, tomato, salt, pepper, garlic powder, and nutritional yeast on top. Mix well.

5. Chill for an hour before serving for best results.

TIPS

- Add 1 cucumber diced and de-seeded.

Ginger Dressing

There have been only a few Sushi restaurants we have been to that make a delicious ginger dressing gluten-free and we savored every bite. I just had to come up with something at home so we could enjoy it more often. I have 2 versions of ginger dressing, one with Miso and one without. Our family loves the fresh ginger bite, we can't get enough of it!

PREP TIME: *15 minutes*   **TOOLS:** *Vitamix, blender, or food processor*

INGREDIENTS

Dressing Without Miso:
4-5 large carrots, peeled
¼ cup rice vinegar
½ cup olive oil (or avocado oil)
1 garlic clove
3 Tbsp ginger (25g)
1 Tbsp tamari or gluten-free soy sauce
½ tsp sesame oil
1 Tbsp raw cane sugar
2 Tbsp cold water

Dressing With Miso:
2 Tbsp miso paste
½ cup rice vinegar
½ cup avocado oil (or extra virgin olive oil)
1 tsp sesame oil
4 large carrots, peeled
1 cloves garlic
1 Tbsp fresh ginger
2 Tbsp cane sugar
½ cup cold water

DIRECTIONS

1. Peel carrots and cut into cubes. You don't need to peel the skin of the ginger, it is safe to eat, but you can remove it if you want to.

2. Add all the other ingredients in the blender or food processor and blend until dressing is smooth.

3. Refrigerate before use for best flavor. Store in the refrigerator for up to a week.

TIPS

- If your carrots aren't that sweet, don't let it stop you from enjoying this dressing. Add more sugar until you get that perfect level of sweet with the spicy from the ginger. I would start with an additional 1 Tbsp of sugar and see if you need to increase from that point.

TWEAKS

_____

_____

Ginger dressing pictured here with smoked sundried tomatoes and pine nuts (pignolia nuts or pinoli).

Epic Caesar Dressing.

Breads

Jen's Gluten-Free Flour Blends

I always have my own version of gluten-free all-purpose flour in the pantry. Whether it is to dust something, dredge your chicken, thicken a gravy, or bake something quickly, having an all-purpose flour on hand makes life a little easier. Yes, of course you can buy gluten-free all-purpose flours at the grocery store and they work great, but I have found that they tend to make certain baked goods drier when I substitute it one-for-one. I wind up having to tweak the recipe to avoid it being too dry. Instead, I always have a large variety of flours and this all-purpose mixture on the ready!

PREP TIME: 5 minutes

INGREDIENTS

White All-Purpose Blend #1:

2 cups brown rice flour
2 cups superfine white rice flour
2 cups tapioca flour
3 tsp xanthan gum

White All-Purpose Blend #2:

2 cups brown rice flour
2 cups sweet sorghum flour
2 cups tapioca flour or arrowroot flour
3 tsp xanthan gum

All-Purpose (Bread) Flour Blend:

1 ⅛ cup tapioca flour
1 ⅛ cup potato starch
1 cup fine brown rice flour
1 cup fine white rice flour
3 tsp xanthan gum

DIRECTIONS

1. In a large mixing bowl, mix very well with a whisk until all the ingredients are well blended. Store in an airtight container.
2. See Kitchen Notes for more information on flours and bread baking "general" rules.

TWEAKS

_____

_____

_____

6 Flour Bread

PREP TIME: 15 minutes   *COOK TIME: 48 minutes*   *OVEN TEMP: 450°*   *TOOLS: 8x4 inch loaf pan*

INGREDIENTS

1 ¼ cup warm water
2 ¼ tsp fast-acting yeast
3 Tbsp turbinado sugar (or cane sugar)
1 cup tapioca flour (or arrowroot flour)

⅓ cup buckwheat flour
⅓ cup amaranth flour
⅔ cup sweet sorghum flour
⅓ cup millet flour
⅓ cup brown rice flour
1 Tbsp xanthan gum

1 tsp salt
3 large eggs
¼ cup extra virgin olive oil (or avocado oil)

DIRECTIONS

1. In a medium mixing bowl, mix together yeast, water, and sugar. Let sit for 5-10 minutes to allow the yeast to bloom.

2. Sift together all the flours, xanthan gum, and salt in a large bowl.

3. When the yeast has bloomed, add it to the large bowl of dry ingredients.

4. Add the eggs and oil. Mix with a hand mixer, stand up mixer or by hand. Make sure you mix until no flour bubbles remain and you have a smooth batter.

5. Cover the bowl with a towel and let it rise for 1 hour.

6. Grease a loaf pan with oil and sprinkle rice flour into it. Discard any excess flour.

7. Place dough into loaf pan and bake at 450°F for 8 minutes. Reduce oven temperature to 350° and bake for another 35-40 minutes.

TWEAKS

_____

_____

_____

_____

_____

_____

_____

_____

Banana Bread with Miso

I know the name of the sweet loaf of bread may be confusing but if you go with me on this one you will not be disappointed! As a matter of fact, this is now the only way I make banana bread. Dairy-free too!

PREP TIME: *15 minutes*   **COOK TIME:** *60-65 minutes*   **OVEN TEMP:** *350°*   **TOOLS:** *(2) 8x4 inch loaf pans*

INGREDIENTS

¼ cup miso paste (I used organic white)

4 bananas, ripe (about 2 cups mashed)

2 ¼ cup Gluten-Free All-Purpose Flour blend (page 77)

¼ cup flax meal

2 tsp psyllium husk powder

1 ½ tsp baking soda

½ tsp baking powder

2 large eggs

1 tsp pure vanilla extract

½ cup coconut oil (can use ghee if you don't mind the dairy)

¼ cup real maple syrup

½ cup brown sugar, firmly packed

Optional (but highly recommended): 1 cup non-dairy chocolate chips

Optional: 1 cup pecans, chopped

DIRECTIONS

1. Grease and lightly flour two loaf pans, making sure to discard any excess flour.
2. In a medium bowl, beat coconut oil, syrup, and brown sugar together.
3. Add bananas and mix.
4. Next add eggs, vanilla, and miso to the mixture and mix again.
5. Sift together a separate bowl: flour, baking soda, baking powder, psyllium husk powder. Mix well.
6. Add the dry ingredients and flax meal to the wet ingredients and mix until all is well blended, scraping down the sides.
7. Mix in chocolate chips or nuts (or both, wink).
8. Pour evenly into the two greased loaf pans and bake in the middle rack of the oven at 350° for 40 minutes. At the 40-minute mark, place a tinfoil "tent" loosely over top of the bread to avoid burning the tops and cook for the remaining time.

TWEAKS

_____

_____

_____

_____

_____

_____

_____

_____

_____

_____

Basic White Bread

This is the recipe that I used for years and years for our three children's lunches. There was no such thing as a school lunch for three kids with Celiac disease, and no gluten-free bread to purchase when this gluten-free lifestyle began for us. We relied heavily on the bread machine to bake bread daily for three growing kids.

PREP TIME: *15 minutes*   **TOOLS:** *8x4 inch loaf pan or bread machine*

INGREDIENTS

Wet ingredients in the bread basket (insert) first:

1 ¼ cup warm water
3 large eggs
¼ cup extra virgin olive oil (or avocado oil)

Next goes the dry ingredients (sifted):

2 Tbsp sugar
1 cup white rice flour
1 cup brown rice flour
1 cup of tapioca starch/flour
1 tsp salt
1 Tbsp xanthan gum

Lastly, on top:

2 ¼ tsp fast-acting yeast

DIRECTIONS

1. Press the "2 pound loaf" selection on your bread machine (or 3 hour bake). I know some machines now have a gluten-free option. I haven't tried it in a long time because my first time was not a success, but I found something that was! I went forward with what worked and never looked back!

No bread machine? No problem! Here are oven directions:

1. Preheat the oven to 425°. Prep Time: 1 hour. Cook Time:55 minutes

2. In a medium mixing bowl mix together yeast, water, and sugar. Let sit for 5-10 minutes to allow the yeast to bloom.

3. Sift together the flours, salt, and xanthan gum.

4. Mix the wet ingredients into the dry and allow the dough to rise for 45 minutes-1 hour, covered with a tea towel. This proofing should allow the bread to rise a bit less than double in size.

5. Grease and flour a loaf pan. Place the dough in the loaf pan and bake at 425° for 10 minutes, then lower the oven temperature to 350° and continue to bake for another 45 minutes.

TIPS

- See kitchen notes (page 24) for tips on making this bread recipe your own!

TWEAKS

_____

_____

_____

_____

_____

_____

Basic White Bread loaf sliced
(pictured on previous page).

Bread in the bread machine
(pictured above).

Texture of the Basic White Bread
(pictured at right).

Buttermilk Cornbread

PREP TIME: 5 minutes   *COOK TIME: 20-25 minutes*   *OVEN TEMP: 400°*   *TOOLS: 9x9 or 8x8 inch baking dish.*

INGREDIENTS

¾ cup Gluten-Free All-Purpose
   Flour blend (page 77)
½ cup almond flour
¾ cup cornmeal
1 cup buttermilk

¼ cup (4 Tbsp) butter, softened
2 large eggs
½ cup packed brown sugar
½ tsp salt

DIRECTIONS

1. Grease your baking dish well with butter.

2. In a mixing bowl, add buttermilk and eggs and mix.

3. In a separate bowl, add all the dry ingredients and mix.

4. Add your dry ingredients to the wet ingredients along with the softened butter. Mix well. Work any lumps out.

5. Add to a greased pan and bake for 20-25 minutes. Will be slightly golden brown and the toothpick will come out clean.

TIPS

- You can use powdered buttermilk. I love to have this on hand at all times you never know when you will need it! I keep it in the refrigerator.

- You can use a hand mixer or a fork works well too.

TWEAKS

_____

_____

_____

_____

_____

_____

_____

_____

Chocolate Zucchini Bread

Zucchini is a wildly versatile vegetable and makes such a delicious loaf of sweet bread while also being the star side dish at dinner.

PREP TIME: 35 minutes   **COOK TIME:** 60-65 minutes   **OVEN TEMP:** 350°   **TOOLS:** (2) 8x4 inch loaf pans

INGREDIENTS

1 ½ cup cane sugar (or turbinado)
1 cup extra virgin olive oil
3 Tbsp unsalted butter
2 Tbsp molasses
1 tsp pure vanilla extract
2 cups Gluten-Free All-Purpose

Flour blend (page 77)
6 Tbsp cacao powder (or cocoa powder)
1 tsp baking soda
½ tsp salt
1 ½ tsp cinnamon

3 eggs
2 large zucchini (or 4 small), grated
Optional: ½-1 cup chopped pecans (pictured on top of the left loaf)
⅔ cups chocolate chips

DIRECTIONS

1. Clean the zucchini skin well. Using a box grater, grate the zucchini.
2. In a medium mixing bowl mix together sugar, olive oil, butter, molasses, and vanilla (can use a hand mixer).
3. In a large mixing bowl, sift together flour, cacao powder, baking soda, salt, and cinnamon.
4. Add the wet ingredients to the dry and mix well.
5. Add the eggs and zucchini and mix until smooth.
6. Grease pans with ghee or butter and spoon the batter into the pans. Bake at 350° for 35 minutes. At the 35 minute mark, "tent" the loafs with tin foil, to avoid burning, and continue cooking.

TIPS

- **Tent the tin foil:** Make a "V" with a long enough piece of tin foil to place loosely over the bread to ensure the top doesn't burn in the final stages of cooking.

- If you don't want to leave the skin on the zucchini that's fine! I keep the skin on because zucchini skin contains lutein and carotenoids, which are both healthy antioxidants.

- **Grating:** The easiest is the box/stand grater, but you can use a hand held. If you want to use a food processor that is fine, but make sure you use the "grating" blade.

- I love using cacao powder when I can in place of cocoa because it adds a tiny bitter twist and tons of health benefits! Who doesn't want the extra vitamins, minerals and antioxidants found in this superfood!

- If you add chocolate chips in, first mix the chips in 2 tsp of gluten-free all-purpose flour, then add to the dough.

Easy Yeast Rolls

This light and airy roll is done in an hour and will add so much to any meal! Upon first taste it was added to the holiday menu by the only "gluten-eater" in the family, my husband. It's that tasty!

PREP TIME: *35 minutes*   **COOK TIME:** *18-20 minutes*   **OVEN TEMP:** *400°*   **TOOLS:** *Muffin pan (12 muffins)*

INGREDIENTS

- 2 ¼ cups Gluten-Free All-Purpose Flour blend (page 77)
- 2 tsp salt
- 2 Tbsp extra virgin olive oil
- 1 large egg
- 1 cup warm water
- 2 Tbsp cane sugar
- 2 ¼ tsp fast acting yeast
- 1 egg white (about 1 Tbsp)

DIRECTIONS

1. In a medium mixing bowl mix together yeast, water, and sugar. Let sit for 5-10 minutes to allow the yeast to bloom.

2. In a separate bowl mix together flour and salt.

3. Add the yeast mixture to the dry mixture along with the egg and oil. Mix together for one minute.

4. Cover the bowl with a towel and let it rise for 30 minutes.

5. Divide the dough evenly among the 12 spots in the muffin pan. Using a large spoon spoon may help as the dough is soft and a bit sticky. Smooth the top and sides with a tiny bit of water on a small spatula for a nicely shaped even looking roll.

6. Lightly brush the top of the dough with the egg white.

7. Bake at 400°F for 20 until the tops are golden brown.

TIPS

- If you don't have the flours to make Jen's Gluten-Free All-Purpose Flour blend but you have a store-bought 1:1 all-purpose flour, the roll may be a bit drier but will still be fantastic!

TWEAKS

_____

_____

_____

_____

_____

_____

_____

_____

_____

_____

_____

_____

Gluten-Free Flour Tortillas

PREP TIME: 15 minutes   *COOK TIME: 25-30 minutes*   *MAKES: 8-10 7-inch round tortillas*

INGREDIENTS

2 ⅓ cup Gluten-Free All-Purpose
   Flour blend (page 77)
1 tsp baking powder
2 tsp brown sugar

1 tsp salt
½-1 cup warm water
¼ cup buckwheat flour
4 Tbsp avocado oil

DIRECTIONS

1. Add all the dry ingredients to a large mixing bowl and mix.

2. Add ½ cup warm water to the dry ingredients and mix well with a fork. Slowly add a tad bit of water at a time until you get a smooth dough. The dough will be perfect when it is not sticky and able to be rolled easily.

3. Form 8-10 balls, about the size of your palm (larger than a golf ball, but smaller than a tennis ball).

4. Sprinkle a liberal amount of buckwheat flour on the counter or a piece of parchment paper and roll out with a rolling pin. To keep that perfect round shape, take a paring knife and cut the edges to make it perfectly round. I personally like the unique shapes that get rolled out.

5. Preheat a cast-iron skillet over medium-high heat. Add some avocado oil and when the oil is hot, add a tortilla to the skillet. Cook for approximately 1-2 minutes or until it has started puffing up and the bottom side is developing those lovely brown spots. Flip the tortilla and cook for another 1-2 minutes.

6. Slide the cooked tortilla onto a covered plate to stay warm and repeat from steps 4 and 5 until you've cooked them all.

7. Serve these warm with your favorite filling!

TIPS

- If you are using a store bought gluten-free all-purpose flour, you may need all of the water and maybe a drizzle more to achieve the consistency you are looking for in this dough.

- If you don't have a cast iron, don't let that stop you! You can use a regular frying pan and still have delicious gluten-free tortillas! Just allow for the tortilla to get lightly browned.

- To roll out the tortilla, instead of buckwheat I have used white rice flour. I just happen to love the taste and hint of color from the buckwheat!

TWEAKS

_____

_____

Focaccia Bread

The kitchen is going to smell so good that everyone will be hanging around waiting for the timer to go off!

PREP TIME: 25-30 minutes   COOK TIME: 30 minutes
OVEN TEMP: Preheat oven to 200° for proofing and 350° for baking   TOOLS: 9x9 inch baking pan

INGREDIENTS

Dry Ingredients:
2 cups brown rice flour
½ cup tapioca starch
½ cup sweet sorghum flour
2 tsp xanthan gum
1 tsp sea salt
1 ¾ cup lukewarm water

2 ¼ tsp active dry yeast (or 1 packet)
2 tsp cane sugar
1 egg, beaten
2 Tbsp extra virgin olive oil, plus more for greasing

Toppings:
2 Tbsp extra virgin olive oil
1 tsp Himalayan salt
1 tsp dried basil
½ tsp dried parsley
½ tsp onion powder
1 tsp granulated garlic powder
1 ½ tsp dried rosemary

DIRECTIONS

1. Whisk together brown rice flour, tapioca starch, sorghum flour, xanthan gum, and sea salt in a bowl.

2. In a separate bowl mix together yeast, water, and sugar. Let sit for 5-10 minutes to allow the yeast to bloom.

3. Preheat the oven to 200° then turn off until temperature is around 70-85°. (See Tips.)

4. In a small bowl, add the olive oil and egg. Beat together.

5. Using either a stand mixer or a hand-held beater, alternate adding the yeast mixture and egg mixture to the dry ingredients until it is all incorporated and smooth.

6. Grease a 9x9 inch baking pan with olive oil.

7. Pour the 2 Tbsp of olive oil on top of the bread, and poke the dough down with the tips of your fingers. Sprinkle all the topping dry ingredients over the top.

8. Place the dough in the warmed oven and allow it to proof for 20 minutes.

9. Remove the bread from the oven, turn the heat up to 350°. Once temperature is reached, place the bread back in to cook for 20 minutes or until golden brown.

TIPS

- Tip on preheating: I love an oven thermometer in my oven. Especially handy with a recipe like this. Most ovens' lowest setting is 200° so unless you are sitting watch the gauge, I suggest allowing the oven to preheat to 200°, turn it off, and walk back to the oven in 5 minutes to see if the temperature is near 85°. Opening the oven will also reduce the temperature a bit.

- Ideal oven proofing temperature is around 70-85°.

- You can use a hand-held mixer or a stand mixer.

- Try some corn meal on the bottom of the dish then pour batter on top.

TWEAKS

_____

_____

_____

_____

_____

High Fiber Bread

Think of a delicious deli sandwich on a hearty earthy bread and this is the bread for you.

PREP TIME: *10 minutes*   **COOK TIME:** *50 minutes*   **OVEN TEMP:** *425°*   **TOOLS:** *9x5 inch loaf pan*

INGREDIENTS

1 ¼ cup slightly warm water
2 ¼ tsp fast-acting yeast
2 Tbsp raw cane sugar or
   turbinado sugar
1 Tbsp guar gum
1 tsp salt

½ cup brown rice flour
¼ cup flax meal
¼ cup millet flour
½ cup sweet sorghum flour
½ cup buckwheat flour
1 cup arrowroot flour

1 Tbsp psyllium husk powder
3 large eggs
¼ cup extra virgin olive oil
⅛ cup pumpkin seeds

DIRECTIONS

1. In a medium mixing bowl mix together yeast, water, and sugar. Let sit for 5-10 minutes to allow the yeast to bloom.

2. In a separate bowl, sift together the guar gum, salt, brown rice flour, flax meal, millet flour, buckwheat flour, arrowroot flour, and psyllium husk powder. Then take a whisk and mix all the ingredients together well.

3. Add the yeast mixture, eggs, and oil to the dry ingredients. Mix well. You can use a mixer, a fork, or a whisk.

4. If your loaf pan is dark or non-stick, sprinkle a little bit of brown rice flour on the bottom. If you are not using a non-stick pan, then lightly grease and flour the pan (be sure to tap out any excess flour).

5. Place dough in the pan. Very lightly wet the top of the loaf with water using a pastry brush then sprinkle the pumpkin seeds on top.

6. Cover with a towel and allow to proof for 30 minutes to 1 hour, until doubled in size

7. Place in the preheated oven for 10 minutes.

8. Lower the oven temperature to 350° and lightly tent with tin foil. Bake for another 40 minutes.

TIPS

- Fiber makes the world a happier place! This loaf has roughly 35 grams of fiber. If you cut 12 slices each slice will roughly be 2.9 grams of fiber!

- Make this recipe in a bread machine: Use 2-pound setting and place wet ingredients in first, then the dry ingredients, and sprinkle yeast on top. "Set and See" your bread in a few hours!

- *For a stronger-flavored loaf with a total of 43 grams of fiber:* Change your flours to the following: ⅓ cup brown rice flour, ⅓ cup flax meal, ⅓ cup quinoa flour, ¾ cup buckwheat flour.

TWEAKS

New York Style Bagels

The taste of this bagel transports me back in time to when I could walk into any deli in New York and grab a quick bagel. This recipe is a true keeper..

PREP TIME: 20 minutes   COOK TIME: 30 minutes   OVEN TEMP: 325°

INGREDIENTS

3 ½ cups Gluten-Free All-
   Purpose (Bread) Flour blend
   (page 77)
½ cup cassava flour
1 tsp xanthan gum

1 tsp psyllium husk powder
1 Tbsp extra virgin olive oil
1 tsp baking soda
1 tsp salt
1 Tbsp fast-acting yeast

2 cups warm water
2 Tbsp sugar
3-4 Tbsp white rice flour for
   kneading and shaping

DIRECTIONS

1. In a medium mixing bowl mix together yeast, water, and sugar. Let sit for 5-10 minutes to allow the yeast to bloom.

2. Add all ingredients to a stand mixer and mix on medium-high until very smooth. Approximately 3-4 minutes.

3. Divide the dough into 8 equal parts (about 126-130 grams each). Shape and knead each portion, using a bit of white rice flour to keep it from sticking, until it comes to a smooth and workable dough. Create a hole in the middle and roll it into a bagel shape.

4. Place each bagel on a parchment-lined baking sheet.

5. Add at least 5-6 cups of water into a pot and wait for it to come to a rolling boil.

6. Place 2 bagels at a time into the boiling water for 10 seconds, flip over for another 10 seconds. Using a large slotted spoon to drain the bagels then place back on the parchment-lined pan.

7. Season the tops of the bagel with what you desire while the bagels are wet, slightly pressing any seasoning into the bagel to help it stick.

8. Boil 5 cups of water and place the water in a roasting pan. Place the pan in a preheated oven of 325°. Place the bagels on the middle shelf in the oven with the roasting pan at the very bottom rack for 10 minutes.

9. Open the oven and purge the steam. Remove the roasting pan of water and leave the bagels in the oven for another 15-20 minutes, until golden brown.

Optional: You can do an oven proof which will get you a larger bagel. I have given this as an option separately because you can make the bagels without this step if you want to shave 30 minutes from the prep time. I have done both and enjoy the bagels both ways.

If you want to proof add the following steps below after step 4. Boil 5 cups of water and place it in a roasting pan. Place the pan on the bottom rack in a preheated oven of 70-85°. Place the bagels in this oven above the roasting pan with water for 30 minutes. Bagels will increase in size to nearly double.

TIPS

- For a smooth bagel, use a bit of the white rice flour and knead each piece a little, then create a cage with your fingers and move the dough in a circle while also pressing lightly onto the dough. You will get a circle, then you can poke the hole in the middle.

- Allow them to cool before cutting.

- When you toast one of these bagels they will get a crunchy exterior which is a perfect pairing to the chewy center.

TWEAKS

_____
_____
_____
_____
_____
_____
_____
_____
_____
_____

Sourdough Starter

I waited 20 years to make my first gluten-free sourdough and I don't want you to wait that long to try it. I read tons of opinions, articles, blogs, and recipes and this is what I came up with. Don't judge yourself! Give the sourdough starter a try and you will be so happy that you did. Begin with brown rice flour and if you find this to be easy and you enjoy making this type of bread then you can branch out to other starters. The best advice I can give is to be patient and a bit forgiving in your learning process. I went from a flour blob starter to a thriving, yeasty starter! Once I told myself there was no wrong way of playing, I became obsessed! Have fun!

INGREDIENTS

Brown rice flour, fine
Filtered water, room temperature

A towel
Mason jar or wide mouth glass jar

A rubber band

DIRECTIONS

1. Weigh out 50 grams of brown rice flour and 50 grams of filtered room temperature water.

2. Mix together well and cover with a towel. Secure towel loosely with a rubber band. I suggest using a wooden spoon for mixing — don't use metal because you don't want to break the glass mason jar with your beautiful starter inside. If you are wondering if I did that, the answer is yes, that did happen. What a mess!

3. Place your starter in a corner of your kitchen that stays relatively warm (between 70° and 80°). The space shouldn't be a drafty area.

4. Every 12 hours, check the starter and if you see bubbling and hooch developing: (1) Pour off hooch and (2) Add 40 grams of brown rice flour and 40 grams water. Mix. Cover. Store in a secure place. Each time your starter is fed it will grow. (When feeding my starter, I no longer measure by weight, instead I go by consistency. I aim for a smooth, roux-like consistency, but not as watery as a slurry.)

5. Use your nose! When you see bubbles throughout your starter and it has a sour smell with a hint of sweet, you have a mature sourdough starter! The perfect sourdough starter may take between 4-10 days and will have doubled in size.

6. Use it in Gluten-Free Sourdough Bread, page 101.

7. Once you have used it and have some remaining in the bottom of the jar, begin the process again. Feed, mix, cover, and repeat daily until it's ready to bake with or store in the refrigerator.

8. When your starter is ready to store in the refrigerator, place a top loosely on the jar and place it in the back of the refrigerator to ensure it doesn't get knocked over. As I have read, and witnessed, the wild yeast will continue to rise just slower, almost like they're sleeping. Continue to feed your starter once a week.

TIPS

- **Have a few starters going at once** because while you need to allow the wild yeast to grow, you are also going to need a decent volume. For example, my recipe calls for 250 grams of mature starter. This can be tricky if you are feeding your starter a little at a time. I always have a backup just in case I want/need a loaf sooner than it will take to build that the volume I need for another loaf of beautiful gluten-free sourdough bread with the perfect wild yeast starter.

- You will soon become a pro at knowing the perfect consistency of your starter. I believe you will also begin to trust your gut with the amount of flour and water added during feedings in order to achieve a smooth consistency that is not too watery like a slurry but more like a roux.

- **I prefer a wide mouth jar, 5.75 inches wide (.75 liter)** because it is easier to mix within the jar and scrape every morsel out when the time comes to use it or transfer it into another jar.

- **Keep a log** of when you fed the starter and how it responded.

- **"Hooch"** is a completely harmless liquid that may form on top of the starter as a result of alcohol that develops

from the yeast fermenting. Some people simply stir it back into the starter and feed the starter, I pour it off before feeding.

- **Keep multiple mason jars available** to mix starter and transfer into clean jars if needed.

- Make sure you have plenty of flour on hand to be able to feed your starter and watch it grow. **Higher protein flour works well for making a sourdough starter.**

- Once your starter is ready to go in the refrigerator, I take a sharpie to the mason jar to note the date of the last feed.

- If you have a good amount of starter, you can pour some off for a friend to begin their own, or start another starter for yourself.

TWEAKS

_____
_____
_____
_____
_____
_____
_____
_____
_____
_____
_____
_____
_____
_____
_____
_____
_____
_____
_____
_____
_____
_____
_____
_____
_____

Sourdough Bread

I'd like to give you a few options on this sourdough bread, from "starter" to finish! You have a large window of prep time in this recipe. Many wonderful bakers use a longer proof. I'm showing you, within this cookbook, my style of cooking and baking and this is how I make this bread. We love this sourdough bread and I use the smaller window of proofing! But you can decide for yourself — I suggest you try both ways. Maybe you will decide you like the shorter time (which is all I do now) and see that it makes a great loaf of artisan sourdough bread in a jiff!

PREP TIME: *2-24 hours*   **COOK TIME:** *55 minutes*   **OVEN TEMP:** *415°*   **TOOLS:** *7-quart Dutch oven (cast iron)*

INGREDIENTS

80g potato starch (not potato flour)
60g tapioca starch/flour
80g sweet sorghum flour
95g brown rice flour
12g sea salt

10g psyllium husk powder
7g fast acting yeast (2 tsp)
20g maple syrup
250g filtered water
250g sourdough starter (brown rice starter)

2 Tbsp brown rice flour (for kneading and dusting, if necessary)

TIPS

- I have done this recipe without yeast and it works great. If you don't care for using yeast, omit!

- Use a scale. I have always avoided using a scale in recipes but, I must confess, this is a recipe that does best when the ingredients are weighed!

- Many people like to do an overnight proof. I prefer my bread faster but I have done an overnight proof several times and here are the steps I used:
  1. Follow all steps in the recipe through and including step 6.
  2. Take the dough out and knead then form back into a tight ball. Cover and allow to rise for one hour. After about 2-5 hours of kneading then rising, the dough should double in size.
  3. Place the dough back into the lightly dusted proofing bowl, then cover tightly with plastic wrap and place in the refrigerator overnight.
  4. The next morning, take the dough out of the refrigerator and allow it to sit on the counter for 1 hour.
  5. Continue on to step 7 in the recipe.

TWEAKS

_____

_____

_____

_____

_____

_____

_____

_____

_____

_____

DIRECTIONS

1. In a medium-sized bowl, add yeast, psyllium husk powder, and water, mix well and let sit for 20 minutes. It will become jelly-like in consistency.

2. In a large mixing bowl, sift together potato starch, tapioca starch, sorghum flour, brown rice flour, and salt.

3. After 20 minutes add the starter to the wet ingredients.

4. **By hand:** Combine the wet ingredients into the dry ingredients. I like to mix it with a dough whisk first then dump the mixture onto my counter. Keep a small amount of extra rice flour on the side only if needed — don't use too much or you will end up with an overly dry dough. Knead the dough until well blended, about 7-10 minutes.

   Stand Mixer: Use a dough hook (or paddle) Mix all ingredients together on low to medium speed for about 4 minutes. The mixer will do most of the kneading for you and form into a ball in the mixing bowl. Next place the dough onto the counter. Knead it by hand to feel the consistency and also work the dough into a proper tight ball.

5. At the end of step 4, your dough should look like a ball. Next you will pull the dough toward yourself with your hand, cupping the ball of dough on the side. You will pull the dough towards you in a dragging motion which will create tension on the outside of the dough and to help make a smooth ball. It should appear smooth without any tears or cracks. You will repeat this process on all sides of the ball until completely smooth all around, creating a boule (a round loaf of crusted bread).

6. Place in a banneton bowl lightly dusted with white rice flour or brown rice flour. If you don't own a banneton, then lightly dust the bottom of a mixing bowl with rice flour. Cover with a towel and place in a warm spot in the kitchen for 45 minutes.

7. Preheat the oven to 415° with the Dutch oven and lid inside.

8. Score the boule with a sharp knife, paring knife, or a bread lame if you have one.

9. When the oven says it has hit the desired temperature, leave the Dutch oven in there for a few more minutes to ensure it is warmed all the way through.

10. Place the scored boule onto a long strip of parchment paper and carefully place it into the preheated (and very hot) Dutch oven. Cover with the lid, and bake for 40 minutes.

11. Remove the lid of the Dutch oven and continue to bake the bread for an additional 25-30 minutes. You are looking for the top and bottom to be golden brown.

12. Allow to cool for 30-45 minutes before cutting.

Mains

Chicken Fajitas
Jen's Fajita Seasoning
Super Chili
Chicken Kebabs and Marinade
Almond-Crusted Cod
Kale and Beans
Black Bean Quinoa Burger
Tuna Casserole
Vegetable Lasagna with
Cashew Cheese
Lemon Chicken
Roasted Chicken You Will Adore
Beef Fajitas with Tahini Sauce

Tahini and Tahini Sauce
Shake It Up Pork Chop
One Dish Wonder Salsa Chicken
Salmon Patties
Shrimp & Arti Hearts
Loaded Meatloaf
Meatballs
Gluten-Free Homemade Pasta
Our Family's Tomato Sauce
The Kids' Favorite Pizza
Pizza Night with Fun Flours
Cauliflower Crust Pizza

Chicken Fajitas

You will be dreaming about this flavorful dish long after it's over. All the sides that you can add will have you savoring each bite.

PREP TIME: 4 minutes   *COOK TIME: 5-8 minutes*

INGREDIENTS

1-1 ½ pounds chicken breasts, sliced thin
1 ½-2 Tbsp avocado oil

⅛ cup Jen's Fajita Seasoning
1 Tbsp lemon juice

DIRECTIONS

1. You can use the same skillet you used to cook your Peppers & Onions (page 46). Take the same hot skillet, add avocado oil, and preheat over a medium flame.

2. Add your sliced chicken breast strips.

3. Cook the chicken and move it around the skillet so you get an even cook on all the pieces.

4. About 4 minutes into the cooking process, add fajita seasoning and stir until chicken is evenly coated.

5. After another 2-3 minutes chicken should be almost done, add the lemon juice and stir into the chicken.

Jen's Fajita Seasoning

INGREDIENTS

3 tsp chili powder
2 tsp salt
½ tsp black pepper
2 tsp paprika
2 tsp sugar
1 ½ tsp fine onion powder
1 tsp fine garlic powder
½ tsp cayenne pepper
2 tsp cumin

DIRECTIONS

1. Mix well and store in a small glass jar for herbs that has a tight top for the next time!

TIPS

• The perfect accompaniment to this recipe is the Fajita Onions (page 46), Peppers & Onions (page 46), sour cream, sharp cheddar cheese, salsa, or Our Special Guacamole (page 45). Don't forget to make the Gluten-Free Flour Tortillas (page 90)!

Super Chili

When we have the whole family of five at home, we make this full recipe and still have leftovers. Don't worry, it's easy to cut this recipe in half.

PREP TIME: 20 minutes   COOK TIME: 2 hours   TOOLS: 8-quart pot

INGREDIENTS

- 2 pounds organic ground turkey
- 1 pound hot Italian turkey (or chicken) sausage
- 8 cloves garlic
- 1 large green pepper (or 2 small)
- 1 large onion (or 2 small)

- 2 (14.5-ounce) cans diced tomato
- 1 (10-ounce) can HOT Ro*Tel
- 2 (15-ounce) cans beans, your choice (I suggest kidney beans, black beans, or pinto beans)
- 1 pack gluten-free chili seasoning

- for 2 pounds of meat (look for GF label)
- 3 Tbsp avocado oil
- 2-3 cups water

DIRECTIONS

1. Use a garlic press and press the garlic, or dice the garlic very small. Dice onion and pepper.

2. Sauté peppers and onions in 2 Tbsp oil. After about a minute, add the garlic. Cook until translucent or beginning to brown. Take off the heat and set aside.

3. Add 1 Tbsp oil to sauce pot. Remove sausage from casing and crumble into pot. Add the ground turkey and brown the meats.

4. Into the same pot, add the vegetables, diced tomatoes, Ro*Tel, tomato paste and seasoning packs.

5. Add 2-3 cups of water and help mix.

6. Cover with lid and allow to simmer for 1 hour or so, stirring occasionally.

7. 30 minutes before you are ready to eat, add the beans. Let it simmer for another 30 minutes with the lid on. Stir occasionally.

TIPS

- Watch the consistency: If its too thick, add a little water. Too loose? Leave the lid off, turn the heat up slightly, and stir often.

- Only have one seasoning packet? Don't fret! Add ¼ tsp of these spices to up the flavor: chili, cumin, coriander, paprika, and ground chipotle.

TWEAKS

_____

_____

108

Chicken Kebabs and Marinade

PREP TIME: 1 hour 25 minutes   COOK TIME: 30-35 minutes   TOOLS: 10-12 skewers

INGREDIENTS

Chicken Marinade:
⅛ cup avocado oil
1 tsp salt
½ tsp pepper
3 Tbsp fresh lemon juice
2 Tbsp red wine vinegar
4 garlic cloves, sliced
1 tsp garlic powder
½ cup diced onions
2 tsp dried parsley
1 tsp paprika

Veggie Marinade:
⅛ cup avocado oil
1 tsp salt
½ tsp pepper
3 Tbsp fresh lemon juice
2 Tbsp red wine vinegar
4 garlic cloves, sliced
1 tsp garlic powder
½ cup diced onions
2 tsp dried parsley
1 tsp paprika

Kebabs:
3-4 pounds chicken breast, cubed
2 zucchini, cut in ½ inch thick slices
1 red bell pepper, cut in 1-2 inch pieces
1 large onion, cut in 1-2 inch pieces
½ red onion, cut in 1-2 inch pieces
1 green bell pepper, cut in 1-2 inch pieces
12-14 small button mushrooms (or 6-7 medium-sized mushrooms cut in half)

DIRECTIONS

For Meat:

1. Add chicken marinade ingredients into a sealable bag (or bowl) and mix well.

2. Cut chicken into 2 inch cubes and into a marinade bag (or bowl).

3. Place the marinating chicken in the refrigerator for an hour.

4. After 1 hour mix the chicken and marinade around then allow to marinate for another hour.

For Vegetables:

5. Cut all the vegetables into 1-2 inch pieces, excluding mushrooms.

6. If mushrooms are small leave them whole, if they are medium/large cut in half.

7. In a separate bowl, add all vegetable marinade ingredients. Pour marinade over vegetables. Place in the refrigerator to marinate for a minimum of 30 minutes or until the grill is ready.

Skewer Directions:

8. Turn the grill on high and allow it to warm up for at least 5 minutes.

9. Place the chicken on a skewer, placing a piece of marinated onion in between each piece. On separate skewers alternate the vegetables in a fun, colorful pattern.

10. Place chicken on the grill, turning when each side has browned (about 2-3 minutes), then lower to medium heat.

11. Place the vegetables on the grill, turning when each side has browned (about 2-3 minutes). Should take around 15 minutes.

TIPS

- If you choose to do meat and veggies on the same skewer, I recommend leaving a small amount of room between the meat and vegetables so that the chicken cooks thoroughly.
- If you are using wooden skewers, place in water and soak for a few minutes before placing food on them and onto the grill.

TWEAKS

_____

_____

Almond-Crusted Cod

PREP TIME: 10 minutes   *COOK TIME: 20-22 minutes*   *OVEN TEMP: 425°*

INGREDIENTS

2 pounds cod
2 large eggs, beaten
2 cups almond flour

1 tsp garlic powder
½ tsp salt
½ tsp cumin

1 tsp coriander
1 tsp dried parsley
1 tsp onion powder

DIRECTIONS

1. Cut the cod into 4 to 6-inch pieces.
2. Mix all the dry ingredients in a bowl.
3. In a smaller mixing bowl beat the eggs.
4. Place a piece of cod at a time into the beaten egg, then add to the dry bowl and coat with the flour mixture. Pat the fish into the mixture to fully coat it. Place coated fish on a parchment-lined baking sheet.
5. Spray the top of the fish with avocado oil spray.
6. Bake at 425° for 20 minutes.

TIPS

- My husband and my oldest daughter like their fish dry so I leave a few pieces in for for an additional 5-8 minutes. I take mine out at the recommended time above.
- This fish is great when paired with fresh lemons or Quick Garlic Aioli (page 39).
- A good accompanying side dish is the Sesame Peas (page 43) or salad with Ginger Dressing (page 71).

TWEAKS

_____
_____
_____
_____
_____

Kale and Beans

PREP TIME: 10 minutes   *COOK TIME: 1 hour*

INGREDIENTS

Kale:
1 pound kale
4 cloves garlic, chopped
½ large sweet onion (1 cup diced)
2 Tbsp extra virgin olive oil
1 tsp Himalayan salt
½ tsp black pepper
4 cups water

Beans:
1 Tbsp extra virgin olive oil
2 (15-ounce) cans cannellini beans
   (reserve liquid from one can)
2 cloves garlic, minced
½ sweet onion (1 cup diced)
½ tsp Himalayan salt
½ tsp black pepper
2 tsp dried parsley

DIRECTIONS

1. In a large sauce pot, sauté cut garlic and onions.
2. When the vegetables are lightly brown, add 4 cups of water to the pot. Reduce heat to simmer.
3. While adding the kale to the pot, remove any large or thick stems.
4. Add in the salt and pepper. Mix well.
5. Bring to a boil, cover and lower to simmer for 45 minutes to 1 hour.

While the Kale is simmering, prepare your beans.

6. In a medium-sized pot add olive oil and sauté onions and garlic until lightly brown.
7. Add the entire contents of one can of beans.
8. Drain the second can of beans and discard the liquid, add beans to the pot.
9. Add salt, pepper, and parsley. Mix well.
10. When the mixture begins to bubble lightly, turn down the heat to medium.
11. After 10 minutes, turn the heat off.
12. When the kale is cooked and tender, you can warm the beans back up for 2-3 minutes.
13. Take a serving of kale and top with the beans!

TIPS

- You can top the kale and beans with red pepper flakes and romano or parmesan cheese. A sharp cheddar cheese will work well too.

- If you want to add even more nutrients to this meal you can replace the water with bone broth.

- Add wild rice, white rice, or Corn Bread (recipe page 85) to this dish and make it a complete protein.

TWEAKS

_____

_____

_____

Black Bean Quinoa Burger

PREP TIME: 30 minutes   *COOK TIME: 30 minutes*   *OVEN TEMP: 375°*

INGREDIENTS

6 large Portobello mushroom caps, diced small
4 cloves garlic, minced
2 Tbsp extra virgin olive oil
15-ounce can black beans, drained
1 ½ cup cooked quinoa
2 large eggs, beaten

½ tsp onion powder
½ tsp salt
½ tsp paprika
½ tsp dried chives
1 tsp dried cilantro
¼ cup + 1 Tbsp gluten-free all-purpose flour

Avocado oil spray
⅛ cup cassava flour
⅛ cup gluten-free all-purpose flour

DIRECTIONS

1. In a large saucepan, sauté mushrooms and garlic in olive oil until mushrooms have reduced in size, about 4-5 minutes.

2. Add drained beans to the pan and mix. Allow to cook for 2 minutes then mash with a meat/potato masher.

3. Into a large bowl add cooked quinoa, mushroom/bean mixture, eggs, onion powder, salt, paprika, chives, cilantro, and flour. Mix well.

4. Allow the mixture to sit for 5 minutes.

5. Form into 6 burgers. Combine ⅛ cup cassava flour and ⅛ cup gluten-free all-purpose flour. Sift flour mixture lightly on top of each burger. Pat down with your fingers.

6. Spray the top of each burger with avocado oil.

7. Sprinkle salt lightly on top of each burger and bake in a preheated oven.

8. Flip after 20 minutes, then bake for another 10 minutes.

TWEAKS

_____

_____

_____

Tuna Casserole

This was the first meal I ever made with my husband while we were still dating. He was skeptical when I told him what I had made, but seeing his face light up when he realized he liked this creation was priceless. It has been a hit ever since that day back in 1990!

PREP TIME: 10 minutes   **COOK TIME:** 25-30 minutes   **OVEN TEMP:** 375°   **TOOLS:** 13x9 inch baking dish

INGREDIENTS

- 4 (4-ounce) cans white meat tuna in water
- 16 ounces dry gluten-free penne pasta (cooked)
- 1 cup diced onion
- 2 cups portobello mushrooms, cut small

- 3 cloves garlic, minced
- 2 Tbsp extra virgin olive oil
- 2 Tbsp butter
- 2 (14-ounce) cans gluten-free cream of mushroom soup
- ½ cup grated parmesan cheese
- 2 Tbsp grated parmesan cheese

- 1 tsp salt
- ½ tsp pepper
- ½ Tbsp dried parsley

DIRECTIONS

1. In large saucepan sauté garlic, onion, and mushrooms in oil and butter until onions are translucent.
2. Transfer to a large mixing bowl.
3. Cook pasta until al dente then drain.
4. Open tuna, drain well, and add to the bowl. Break up the tuna really well (using gloved hands may be easiest).
5. Next add soup, ½ cup parmesan cheese, and pasta. Mix well.
6. Place in a large baking dish and top with 2 Tbsp parmesan cheese.
7. Cook for 25-30 minutes until golden brown on top!

TWEAKS

_____

_____

_____

Vegetable Lasagna with Cashew Cheese

Over a decade ago I found a recipe for a vegan lasagna that said to sauté all the vegetables together in a pot. While my family does enjoy a good vegetable dish, they have never been fans of mushy veggies. I tackled this idea my way; honoring each vegetable's threshold to mush and adding flavor to each layer. I found that maintaining a good texture for each vegetable together with the "cheese" sauce I created made a beautiful combination. While this recipe has a bit more prep, I cannot stress to you how much the effort is worth. It was such a hit that I can promise the next time you make it you will double it!

PREP TIME: 1 hour   COOK TIME: 30 minutes   OVEN TEMP: 400°   TOOLS: 13x9 inch baking dish

INGREDIENTS

2 green zucchini, sliced on an angle ½ inch thick

1 yellow zucchini, sliced on an angle ½ inch thick

1 medium sweet onion, diced

3 leeks, chopped (see Tips)

4 ounces baby kale

6 ounces spinach

4-5 cups swiss chard (about 1 bushel)

5 cups of broccoli, chopped small

4 cups of cauliflower, chopped small

2-3 Tbsp extra virgin olive oil

2 cloves garlic, minced

1-2 cups water

Salt and pepper, to taste

1 Tbsp garlic powder

Cashew "Cheese":

3 cups cashews soaked in water for at least 30 minutes

3 lemons, juiced

2 tsp garlic powder

2 tsp salt

3 heaping Tbsp miso paste

DIRECTIONS

1. Clean and cut all the veggies according to the ingredient list.

2. Into a large saucepan add 1 Tbsp olive oil and minced garlic. Lightly brown the garlic then add in your greens: spinach, kale and beet greens. Mix until well combined and cook until wilted, about 5 minutes. Once cooked, remove from the pan and set aside. Season lightly with salt and pepper.

3. Into a large saucepan add 1 Tbsp olive oil, leeks, and onion. Sauté until onions begin to appear translucent, about 4-5 minutes. Sprinkle with salt, pepper, and 1 tsp garlic powder. Remove from pan and set aside in a separate bowl from the greens.

4. Into a large sauce pot add broccoli and ½ cup water. Allow to steam (about 5-6 minutes). Season with salt, pepper, and 1 tsp garlic powder. Remove from the pan and set aside. If you can fit both broccoli and cauliflower in a large sauce pot then great! Allow for a bit more time, around 8-10 minutes, to ensure all the veggies become slightly steamed yet still crunchy.

5. Into a large sauce pot add cauliflower and ½ cup water. Allow to steam (about 5-6 minutes). Season with salt, pepper, and 1 tsp garlic powder. Remove from the pan and set aside.

6. Into a large saucepan or two add sliced zucchini. Allow for some room so zucchini can touch the pan. Add in a few drops of water, no more than 1 Tbsp. The goal is to begin to cook them but not let them become translucent. Cook for about 4 minutes depending on how thick or thin you cut the zucchini pieces.

7. Add all sauce ingredients into a Vitamix or a blender and blend until smooth.

Layering the Lasagna:

8. Layer the lasagna into the baking dish either in your own way or following the order below:

   Bottom layer: a layer of zucchini
   Second layer: cashew "cheese" sauce
   Third layer: greens
   Fourth layer: broccoli and cauliflower
   Fifth layer: cashew "cheese" sauce
   Sixth: leeks and onions
   Seventh: cashew "cheese" sauce

9. Bake for 30 minutes until you can see bubbling on the sides. The cashew "cheese" may even become slightly brown! Perfection!

TIPS

- Leeks: Clean leeks thoroughly as these are dirty little buggers. I slice down the middle first, rinse thoroughly, cut down the middle, then cut into crescent-shaped slices.

- Have left over veggies and "cheese"? Fantastic! You can make a smaller baking dish with what is left. You will be happy you did because once the last bite is gone you will be planning your next batch!

- I use a variety of vegetables in this recipe each time. But my favorite "Go-To's" are: zucchini, onion, leek, cauliflower, kale, spinach, broccoli, and swiss chard. Others vegetable I have used in this recipe when the above aren't available or I have them on hand include beet greens, mushroom scallions, mustard greens, pepper, and green beans.

Lemon Chicken

PREP TIME: 35 minutes   *BAKE TIME: 35-40 minutes*   *OVEN TEMP: 350°*   *TOOLS: 10x15 inch baking dish*

INGREDIENTS

2 pounds chicken breast
1 cup fresh squeezed lemon juice
1 cup Gluten-Free All-Purpose
  Flour blend (page 77)

½ tsp garlic powder
½ tsp onion powder
½ tsp salt
½ tsp black pepper

1-2 Tbsp salted butter
1-2 Tbsp extra virgin olive oil
2-3 Tbsp chicken broth

DIRECTIONS

1. Into a plastic sealable bag (or bowl) add flour, garlic powder, onion powder, salt, and pepper. Mix well.

2. Cut chicken breast in half down the middle.

3. Place chicken in between pieces of cling film or parchment paper, then place on a cutting board. Pound covered meat with a meat tenderizer.

4. Add pounded chicken to the flour mixture, coat with mixture, and shake any excess flour off.

5. To a large frying pan add 1 Tbsp butter and 1 Tbsp olive oil over a medium-high flame. Once the butter and oil are hot, gently place several pieces of chicken into the pan. Allow a little space in between each piece. Cook for 2-3 minutes per side (depending on thickness). *Not all the chicken will fit in one pan.*

6. Add chicken broth to the pan, cover, and steam for 2 minutes.

8. Pour 3-4 Tbsp lemon juice over the chicken. Move it around and flip to both sides, coating chicken fully in lemon juice.

9. Into your baking dish, add all pieces of chicken and pour any remaining lemon juice and pan drippings onto the chicken. Repeat with remaining chicken.

10. Bake in the oven for 20 minutes until fully cooked.

TIPS

- If you would like to omit the chicken broth step, you can replace it by using more butter and oil.

- You can fully cook these chickens in the frying pan if you like, but I personally prefer par cooking them and finishing them off in the oven.

Roasted Chicken You Will Adore

PREP TIME: 10 minutes   ROAST TIME: 2 hours 45 minutes   OVEN TEMP: 350°   TOOLS: Large roasting pan

INGREDIENTS

4 ½ pound whole chicken
½ tsp Himalayan salt
¼ tsp black pepper
½ tsp onion powder

½ tsp garlic powder
½ tsp dried parsley (pinch between fingers to make finer)
1 whole onion, quartered

2 stalks celery, halved
Optional: 1 lemon, halved

DIRECTIONS

1. Mix all the dry ingredients together in small bowl or ramekin.

2. Cut celery, onion, and optional lemon.

3. Place your finger, or a knife, under the skin of the chicken and separate the skin from the meat. It is optional to trim off any excess fat.

4. Season the chicken. Sprinkle the dry seasoning mixture under the skin, on the bottom of the chicken, and liberally over the top of the skin, thighs, and wings.

5. Place as much of the onions, celery, and optional lemon in the cavity as possible; there may not be room for all of it. If you have two chickens, like I have shown, I placed ½ the onion and all the celery in one, and the other ½ of onion and the lemon in the second.

6. Bake chicken in a roasting pan. Set your timer for 2 hours and 40 minutes and check your chicken's internal temperature with a meat thermometer. You are going to want 165°. Check that the temperature has been reached in all areas of the chicken.

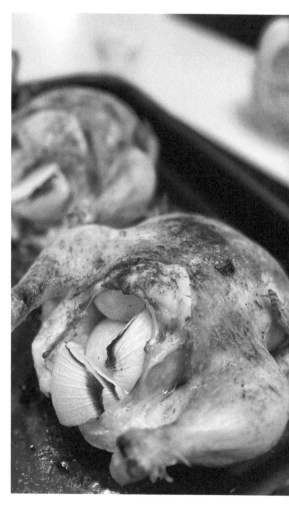

TIPS

- You can add heat like cayenne pepper or paprika to the seasoning.

- Embrace roasted chicken nights knowing that there will be chicken salad and a delicious Bone Broth (recipe page 57) in your future.

- Adding a lemon to the cavity brings moisture and flavor.

- A general rule of thumb for roasting a chicken is to cook it for 25 minutes per pound. Of course, if you are using a convection oven the time will go faster.

- If you want to use a 400° oven you will have a faster cooking time but you will need to watch that the skin doesn't burn. Use a tented piece of aluminium foil over the top to avoid burning.

Beef Fajitas with Tahini Sauce

This is a true melting pot of flavor. West Texas and Northern Mexico pair with the Middle East, bringing these flavors together to make one heck of a tasty meal. Pair with Tahini Sauce (page 126).

PREP TIME: 5 hours 25 minutes   COOK TIME: 15 minutes   TOOLS: 3-quart pan

INGREDIENTS

Beef:
1 ¼- 1 ½ pounds beef top round, cut in ¼- ½ inch thin strips
2 Tbsp dried sliced garlic
2 tsp garlic powder
1 tsp onion powder
¼ cup avocado oil
1 lemon, juiced

Vegetables:
Jen's Fajita Seasoning (page 107)
1 zucchini, cut into strips
1 broccoli crown, chopped
1 red bell pepper, cut into strips
½ yellow bell pepper, cut into strips
½ large onion, sliced

12 brussel sprouts, thinly sliced
Avocado oil
Water

DIRECTIONS

1. Add 2 Tbsp oil to pan and sauté peppers, broccoli, and brussels sprouts. About 1 minute into the process add 2 Tbsp water and stir the vegetables often to get an even steam. Sprinkle evenly with Jen's Fajita Seasoning, then cook another 4-5 minutes. Set aside. You may need to sauté and steam the vegetables in two batches.

2. Add 2 Tbsp oil to the pan and add onions and zucchini. Sprinkle evenly with Jen's Fajita Seasoning. Sauté another 3-4 minutes until the texture that is cooked but not mushy. Set aside.

3. Add oil to pan, make sure it is hot, then add the beef and sprinkle evenly with Jen's Fajita Seasoning. Stir around in the frying pan flipping the beef strips. Beef should be done in about 3-4 minutes.

TIPS

• Try it out with a side of Tahini Sauce! Delicious combo of flavors!

TWEAKS

_____

_____

_____

_____

_____

_____

_____

_____

_____

_____

Tahini and Tahini Sauce

PREP TIME: 20 minutes

INGREDIENTS

Tahini:
½ cup extra virgin olive oil
2 cups organic sesame seeds
(hulled)
½ tsp salt
Up to ¼ cup (4 Tbsp) cold water

Tahini Sauce:
2 large cloves garlic
½ cup lemon juice
½ tsp Himalayan salt
¼ tsp cumin
½ cup tahini
3 Tbsp cold water

DIRECTIONS

Tahini:

1. Add sesame seeds, oil, and 1 Tbsp cold water to a blender, food processor, or mortar and pestle and blend. You are trying to make this into a smooth, creamy texture.
2. Gradually add water until you achieve the consistency you desire. You may need all the water.
3. You can add more oil as well until the tahini is more liquid if that is your preference.

Tahini Sauce:

1. Using a hand blender or small food processor add all the ingredients into a bowl and blend for 30 seconds-1 minute until silky smooth.

Shake It Up Pork Chop

PREP TIME: 5 minutes   *COOK TIME: 24 minutes*   *OVEN TEMP: 375°*

INGREDIENTS

4 pork chops (about 1- 1 ½ inches thick)
⅔ cups gluten-free bread crumbs
⅓ cup almond flour

½ tsp salt
¼ tsp pepper
½ tsp paprika
½ tsp garlic powder

1 egg
2 ½ Tbsp avocado oil, divided

DIRECTIONS

1. Add all the dry ingredients to a sealable plastic bag and mix well.

2. Add ½ Tbsp avocado oil to the bag, seal and smash around in your fingers until oil is well dispersed in the dry ingredients.

3. Beat one egg in a medium-sized bowl.

4. Dredge your pork chops in the beaten egg then place in the bag. Move the pork chop around in the bag to coat it really well.

5. Remove the pork chop from the bag and set aside on a plate. Repeat with the rest of the pork chops.

6. When all the pork chops are coated, heat up 2 Tbsp avocado oil in a cast iron frying pan. When oil is hot, place the pork chops in the pan and cook 2 minutes each side until golden brown.

7. If your frying pan is oven safe, place it directly into the oven for 18-20 minutes (depending on the pork chop thickness). If not, add pork chops to a parchment-lined sheet before baking.

TWEAKS

_____

_____

_____

TIPS

- Pork chops are done when internal temperature reaches 145°.

One Dish Wonder Salsa Chicken

Perfect meal for the night that you want it all but don't have all the time in the world!

PREP TIME: 15 minutes   **COOK TIME:** 55 minutes   **OVEN TEMP:** 350°   **TOOLS:** 10x15 inch baking dish

INGREDIENTS

- 2 pounds chicken breast, cut into ½ inch cubes
- 2 Tbsp extra virgin olive oil, divided
- 1 jar (10-12 ounces) salsa
- 1 medium sweet onion, diced
- 8 cups spinach
- 2 cups chicken or bone broth
- 16 ounces frozen broccoli florets (or cuts)
- 1 cup uncooked quinoa
- 8 ounces sharp cheddar cheese, shredded
- 2 tsp fine garlic powder
- 2 cups water

DIRECTIONS

1. Sauté onion in 1 Tbsp olive oil in a saucepan until onion is lightly translucent.
2. Add the spinach to the saucepan. Add 1 tsp of fine garlic powder. Stir until spinach is wilted, then set aside.
3. Place broccoli and quinoa into a 10x15 inch baking dish baking dish and spread evenly.
4. Pour 2 cups of broth evenly over the top of the broccoli and quinoa, then drizzle 1 Tbsp olive oil on top.
5. Add the sautéed spinach, onion, and diced pieces of chicken cuts evenly into the baking dish. Spread the salsa on top.
6. Bake in a preheated 350° oven uncovered for 40 minutes.
7. After 40 minutes, take out of oven, sprinkle shredded cheese on top then bake for an additional 15 minutes. This dish is done when the bottom is bubbly and the cheese is melted and beginning to brown slightly.

TIPS

- Make it hot and spicy with a salsa that brings the heat!
- If you are looking to cut down on sodium, use unsalted chicken broth. As always, if you want more salt, add as you prefer.
- I have used fresh broccoli for this. Remember, frozen broccoli brings in moisture to help cook the quinoa. If you plop fresh broccoli in there you may need a bit more liquid. Add ¼ cup water or broth!

TWEAKS

_____

_____

Salmon Patties

Salmon Patties are such a hit in our family that the kids (who are all grown up and living on their own) found a way to make them even while they were at college. Even today they still make Salmon Patties in their own homes!

PREP TIME: 30 minutes   **COOK TIME: 35-45 minutes**   **OVEN TEMP: 400°**

INGREDIENTS

Salmon:
3 pounds sockeye salmon, fresh
  or frozen
1 Tbsp avocado oil
1 ½ tsp garlic powder
⅛ cup brown sugar (or honey)
1 Tbsp tamari sauce (or gluten-
  free soy sauce)

Breadcrumb Mixture:
4 celery stalks, diced (about
  1 ¾-2 cups)
2 medium-large carrots, diced
  (about 1 cup)
1 large onion, diced (2 cups)
1 tsp garlic powder
2 tsp dried parsley

1 tsp salt
1 tsp pepper
1 cup mayonnaise
2 cups gluten-free breadcrumbs
  (fine)
2 Tbsp extra virgin olive oil (or
  avocado oil)
Avocado oil spray

DIRECTIONS

1. Place salmon on a parchment-lined baking sheet and drizzle oil and tamari sauce on the fish. Then sprinkle sugar and garlic powder on top.

2. Bake salmon in the oven at 400° for 15 minutes (fresh) or 25 minutes (frozen).

3. While the fish is cooking and cooling, cut the celery, carrots, and onion and sauté them all together in a large saucepan with 2 Tbsp olive oil. Once cooked, set aside in a large mixing bowl.

4. Using a fork, flake the salmon. Place pieces in the bowl, ensuring you remove any pin bones (see Tips).

5. Add garlic powder, parsley, salt, pepper, mayonnaise and half of the breadcrumbs to the flaked salmon and mix well. I find it easier to use my gloved hands in this process.

6. Slowly add the remaining breadcrumbs. Your goal is to get the perfect sticky consistency that will enable you to form a 5 ounce ball (about 3 inches wide) that easily stays together. Form the balls, then place them on two parchment-lined baking sheets and press down to form patties.

7. Generously spray the tops with avocado spray and bake at 400° for 20 minutes.

Optional: My gang loves a very golden brown patty with crunch! So we add 3-4 minutes of broil time which we watch very closely. I serve it with tons of lemon for me and YumYum sauce and Sriracha for others.

TWEAKS

_____

_____

_____

TIPS

- If you have bread crumbs that are more like panko, place them in a blender and pulse for a few seconds. I use my Vitamix.

- Pin bones are long, thin bones that run along the length of the fish. They are edible and usually pass through digestion without a problem but they are easy to remove. They may have been removed for you by the store or fish monger. If not, and you are using fresh salmon, you can remove them with needle nose pliers! Pull toward the direction of where the head of the fish would be, or away from the tail.

- If you get frozen salmon, like me, I usually do my "pin bone" search before I begin "flaking" the salmon using your fingers to feel. Once cooked, they're easy to pull out.

- I love to keep frozen wild caught sockeye salmon in my freezer at all times! I'm always ready for a delicious nutrient packed meal that everyone loves.

- These patties are so tasty as left-over! They warm up beautifully in a frying pan or cast-iron skillet.

Shrimp & Arti Hearts

I make this recipe with frozen, wild caught shrimp or fresh shrimp. I began making Shrimp & Arti Hearts (along with scallops) for my husband for our first wedding anniversary, before our kiddos were even born. I continued to make it more than just once a year because it was too good to wait for!

PREP TIME: 20 minutes   **COOK TIME: 20 minutes**

INGREDIENTS

2 pounds shrimp (1 ½ pounds once deveined, deshelled, and defrosted if using frozen)
1 large onion, diced
5 cloves garlic, minced
5-6 Tbsp fresh lemon juice, divided

2 cans artichoke hearts, drained
5 Tbsp extra virgin olive oil, divided
2 tsp dried parsley, divided
4 Tbsp butter, divided
¼ cup cooking sherry (or white wine), divided

5 cups baby spinach (10-16 ounces)
Gluten-free fettuccine or linguine, cooked according to package directions

DIRECTIONS

1. Dice onions, mince garlic, and squeeze lemons.
2. Set aside a small portion of garlic and onions to cook with shrimp.
3. Defrost (if needed), devein, and deshell shrimp.
4. Strain the artichoke hearts and cut into quarters.
5. Into a large saucepan add 3 Tbsp olive oil, onions, garlic, and sauté.
6. Once onions are soft (about 2 minutes) add the artichoke hearts. Season with 1 tsp dried parsley, ¼ tsp salt, 2 Tbsp butter, 2 Tbsp sherry, and 2 Tbsp lemon juice. Continue to cook for 3-4 minutes.
7. Add the spinach, allow to wilt, then set aside.
8. Into a large saucepan add 2 Tbsp olive oil then add shrimp. Season shrimp with 1 tsp dried parsley, ¼ tsp salt, 3 Tbsp Sherry, 2 Tbsp butter, and 3 Tbsp lemon juice. Continue to cook for 3-4 minutes.
9. Combine all the ingredients together into one pan and cook for 2-3 minutes.
10. Top your cooked pasta with this delicious shrimp and artichoke mixture and serve with parmesan cheese.

TWEAKS

_____

_____

_____

_____

_____

_____

_____

_____

_____

_____

_____

Loaded Meatloaf

Why make a plain meatloaf when you can have one packed with flavor as well as vegetables! When I first became a mother, our first-born hated vegetables (ironic because she is now a vegetable fiend). I would steam mixed vegetables and puree them then use them as the binding agent in this Loaded Meatloaf. I'd serve her meatloaf sticks. If she could hold the food in her hand, dunk it in ketchup, and not see a distinct vegetable, all was well. Eventually time gave way to a more lenient toddler. And so, the packed meatloaf was born!

PREP TIME: 25-30 minutes   **COOK TIME: 35-40 minutess**   **OVEN TEMP: 425°**

INGREDIENTS

2 pounds ground turkey
1 pound ground beef (80/20)
3 cups frozen spinach
1 medium onion, diced
4 medium celery stalks, diced

2 large carrots, diced
3 large eggs
1 ½ Tbsp Worcestershire sauce
2 cups cheddar cheese, shredded
½ tsp garlic powder

1 tsp dried parsley
1 "boil in bag" brown rice, uncooked (see Tips).
½ tsp salt
¼ tsp black pepper

DIRECTIONS

1. Cut vegetables and add to large mixing bowl.
2. Place the frozen spinach in the microwave for 1-2 minutes, until defrosted. Squeeze out excess water before adding to the vegetable bowl.
3. Crack the eggs into a small bowl and beat. Add to the large bowl.
4. Add Worcestershire sauce, cheddar cheese, garlic powder, parsley, uncooked brown rice, salt, and pepper. Mix.
5. Add meats to the bowl and mix very well. Onto two parchment-lined baking sheets, form 4 equally-sized round meatloaves. They cook fast this way and are fun!
6. Bake meatloaves at 425° for 35-40 minutes.

TIPS

- Try frozen turnip greens in this recipe. (Defrost in the microwave and add to the meat mixture.) Delicious!

- I have also substituted the "boil in bag" dry rice with either 1 ½ cup of bread crumbs, pre-cooked quinoa, or pre-cooked wild rice!

- If you decide you want 1 large meatloaf instead of 4 smaller ones, then I would lower the temperature to 375° and increase the cook time to 1 hour.

TWEAKS

Meatballs

For a long time I made these meatballs with equal parts ground pork and beef, but as I made changes for my own health needs, I adjusted the recipe. Feel free to make tweaks yourself with ground pork, beef, and/ or turkey to achieve your very own family favorite meatballs!

PREP TIME: 16-18 minutes   *BAKE TIME: 30 minutes*   *OVEN TEMP: 350°*

INGREDIENTS

- 2 pounds ground turkey (or 80/20 ground beef)
- 2 large eggs
- ¾ cup onion or ½ of a large onion, minced
- 2 tsp garlic powder
- 2 Tbsp dried parsley
- ½ tsp salt
- ½ tsp black pepper
- ½ cup gluten-free bread crumb
- ¼ cup grated parmesan cheese

DIRECTIONS

1   Add all ingredients to a bowl and mix well. I like to put gloves on and knead and mix it with my hands until well incorporated.

2. Shaping the balls: The size of the ball you want determines the time needed in the oven. If you choose a very small meatball, you will need less baking time. For example, a meatball made of approximately ¼ cup of meat mixture will need about 30 minutes to bake.

3. Bake for 30 minutes until golden and slightly crunchy!

TIPS

- Two batches of meatballs are pictured, one made only of turkey and the other only beef.

- Want to make this dairy-free? Remove the cheese but increase the salt by ½ -1 tsp.

- If you use ground turkey breast (which is different from ground turkey because it is only turkey breast meat) your meatballs will be dry. I suggest either adding a bit more cheese or spraying the meatballs with oil before baking. You can even throw them in pasta sauce for a bit!

TWEAKS

_____

_____

_____

_____

_____

Homemade Gluten-Free Pasta

PREP TIME: 50 minutes
COOK TIME: 3-4 minutes

INGREDIENTS

2 cups gluten-free all-purpose
   flour
4 Tbsp tapioca flour
1 Tbsp extra virgin olive oil
½ tsp salt
⅓ cup warm water, plus more if
   needed
2 eggs
2 egg yolks

DIRECTIONS

1. Add flours and salt to a bowl and mix.

2. Carefully dump the flour mixture into a pile on the counter and make a hold in the middle.

3. In a small bowl, beat together the eggs, egg yolk, water, and olive oil.

4. Slowly pour the egg mixture into the well in the flour pile while mixing the two together with a fork. Once all the wet ingredients have been added, slowly bring in more of the flour mixture from the sides of the well. Continue to incorporate until you can no longer use the fork.

5. Begin kneading the dough. The goal is to get a well incorporated dough that is smooth. Knead for about 8-10 minutes. Keep a small cup of warm water near you to add if necessary while kneading. I also like to keep a pile of flour on my work surface in case I need to use it.

6. Wrap the dough with a towel or plastic wrap and allow to sit for 20-30 minutes.

7. Roll out the dough with a rolling pin. Once the dough is rolled out into a thin sheet, easily make pasta by cutting thin strips with a knife or pizza cutter. Or if you have a pasta maker, use that and have some fun!

8. Bring a pot of salted water to a rolling boil. Boil pasta for 3-4 minutes depending on how thin your pasta dough was rolled out and how thick you decided to make your noodles.

TIPS

- Use plain white rice flour to dust on top of the pasta once cut to keep it from sticking together. Do not use the same gluten-free all-purpose flour to sprinkle as it makes the pasta have a "gluey" consistency when boiled.

TWEAKS

_____

_____

_____

_____

Our Family's Tomato Sauce

Call it tradition or call it a quirk, but I just think the sauce is better when I use a wooden spoon to stir, just like both my grandmothers used to do! Do you love the smell of sauce simmering in the kitchen? I adore it and I find the longer I allow the sauce simmer the richer the flavors are. I have left this sauce to simmer all day — just like I remember from childhood.

PREP TIME: 15-20 minutes   COOK TIME: Minimum 1 hour   TOOLS: 8-quart sauce pot

INGREDIENTS

¼ cup extra virgin olive oil
8-10 cloves garlic, minced
6-ounce can tomato paste
1 cup water

3 (28-ounce) cans crushed
  tomatoes
20 fresh basil leaves
½ Tbsp dried parsley

2 tsp onion powder
½ Tbsp salt
½ tsp black pepper

DIRECTIONS

1. Add oil, garlic, and tomato paste to the pot. On medium to high heat brown the garlic. Stir the mixture constantly to ensure you don't burn the garlic. With your spoon, move the paste around in the oil and garlic like you are frying it.

2. Pour the cans of tomato sauce into the pot. (Pour 1 cup of water into one of the empty crushed tomato cans and swish it around. Pour the contents into the next empty can and repeat. Then pour into the pot.)

3. Mix sauce well. Add basil, parsley, salt, pepper, and onion powder. Mix again. Allow to come to a boil, cover and turn the heat down to a simmer.

4. Allow the sauce to simmer for a minimum of 1 hour. You will need to stir occasionally.

TIPS

- If you are going to try to let this sauce simmer all day long, add some meat! Chicken breast, pieces of beef or pork, or even your pre-made meatballs!

- A good quality olive oil makes all the different in your cooking and especially in your homemade sauce.

- You can replace a can of crushed tomatoes with a can of diced tomatoes for a chunkier sauce.

- Sauce is good in the refrigerator for up to 7 days. It freezes wonderfully to use in other dishes. I have defrosted and added oregano and used it for a pizza sauce.

TWEAKS

_____

_____

The Kids' Favorite Pizza

This recipe has been our kids' favorite since the early days of our gluten-free life — and it is still asked for to this day! This pizza crust does use shortening, but if you'd like to "tweak" this recipe and make it "cleaner" turn to my favorite "healthier" pizza crust recipe on the next page.

PREP TIME: *20-65 minutes*　　　**BAKE TIME:** *22-28 minutes*　　　**OVEN TEMP:** *400°*　　　**TOOLS:** *Stand mixer*

INGREDIENTS

2 cups rice flour
2 cups tapioca flour
3 ½ tsp xanthan gum
1 tsp salt

2 Tbsp active dry yeast
1 cup lukewarm water
1 Tbsp sugar
3 Tbsp shortening

1 cup warm water
½ cup hot water
4 egg whites, room temperature

DIRECTIONS

1. Into the bowl of a stand mixer add the rice flour, tapioca flour, xanthan gum, and salt.

2. In a separate bowl combine the yeast, sugar, and 1 cup of warm water. Stir together briefly then allow the yeast to bloom for about 5 minutes.

3. In another bowl add the shortening and ½ cup of hot water. Allow to sit to soften the shortening.

4. With the stand mixer on low, pour in the hot water/shortening. Let mix for 30 seconds.

5. Add the egg whites to the stand mixer and continue to mix on low for 30 seconds.

6. Pour the yeast mixture into the bowl of the stand mixer slowly. Make sure to scrape the sides and get all the yeast and sugar into the bowl. Beat on high speed for 4 minutes. (Should look like a spider web against the sides of the bowl.)

7. Sprinkle a small amount of rice flour onto the counter then knead the dough until smooth. Shape into a ball, place back in the bowl, and cover with a towel to let rise for 30-45 minutes. (See Tips.)

8. Divide the dough in half and roll out the dough to the desired pizza size. Add pizza dough to a pizza stone or parchment-lined baking sheet. Bake at 400° degrees for 8 minutes.

9. Take out the crust and add any sauce or toppings. Bake for another 14-20 minutes.

TIPS

- It's all up to you! If you have the time, you can allow the dough to rise for 30-45 minutes. If you want that pizza and don't allow for rise time, no worries, it will still make a delicious pie!

- Brush the crust with olive oil and then sprinkle with granulated garlic for some extra flavor.

TWEAKS

_____

_____

_____

_____

Pizza Night with Fun Flours

This dough makes a delicious crust packed with protein and fiber that will elevate your pizza night!

PREP TIME: 20-65 minutes   **BAKE TIME:** 22-28 minutes   **OVEN TEMP:** 400°   **TOOLS:** Stand mixer

INGREDIENTS

1 cup tapioca flour
1 cup arrowroot flour
1 cup buckwheat
½ cup brown rice flour
½ cup amaranth

½ cup sorghum flour
3 ½ tsp xanthan gum
1 tsp salt
2 Tbsp active dry yeast
1 cup lukewarm water

1 Tbsp sugar
3 Tbsp extra virgin olive oil
2 large eggs, room temperature
2 egg whites, room temperature

DIRECTIONS

1. Into the bowl of a stand mixer add the tapioca flour, arrowroot flour, buckwheat, brown rice flour, amaranth flour, sorghum flour, xanthan gum, and salt.

2. In a separate bowl combine the yeast, sugar, and 1 cup of warm water. Stir together briefly then allow the yeast to bloom for about 5 minutes.

4. With the stand mixer on low, pour in the olive oil. Let mix for 30 seconds.

5. Add the eggs and egg whites to the stand mixer and continue to mix on low for 30 seconds.

6. Pour the yeast mixture into the bowl of the stand mixer slowly. Make sure to scrape the sides and get all the yeast and sugar into the bowl. Beat on high speed for 4 minutes. (Should begin to form into a ball in the bowl.)

7. Sprinkle a small amount of rice flour onto the counter then knead the dough a small amount. This dough doesn't require a lot of kneading. Shape into a smooth ball, place back in the bowl, and cover with a towel to let rise for 30-45 minutes. (See Tips.)

8. Divide the dough in half and roll out the dough to the desired pizza size. Add pizza dough to a pizza stone or parchment-lined baking sheet. Bake at 400° degrees for 8 minutes.

9. Take out the crust and add any sauce or toppings. Bake for another 14-20 minutes.

TIPS

- It's all up to you! If you have the time, you can allow the dough to rise for 30-45 minutes. If you want that pizza and don't allow for rise time, no worries, it will still make a delicious pie!

- Brush the crust with olive oil and then sprinkle with granulated garlic for some extra flavor.

- This dough will have a slightly different feel and consistency than the previous pizza.

TWEAKS

_____

_____

_____

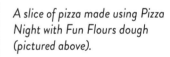

A slice of pizza made using Pizza Night with Fun Flours dough (pictured above).

A slize of pizza made using Cauliflower Crust dough (pictured at left).

Cauliflower Crust Pizza

If you're looking for a lower-carb pizza night that is also dairy-free, then your search is over!

PREP TIME: 5 minutes   **COOK TIME:** 1 hour 25 minutes   **OVEN TEMP:** 350°

INGREDIENTS

1 medium head cauliflower, stems removed
¼ cup buckwheat flour
¼ cup Gluten-Free All-Purpose Flour blend (page 77)

1 Tbsp psyllium husk powder
½ teas salt
½ tsp onion powder
½ tsp garlic powder
3 large eggs

DIRECTIONS

1. Clean the outside of the cauliflower and remove most of the bulky stems.

2. Place cauliflower florets in a food processor. Pulse until the florets are broken into crumbly, rice-sized pieces or smaller. (Makes approximately 5 cups of riced cauliflower.)

3. Spread the riced cauliflower evenly onto a parchment-lined baking sheet. Bake for 20 minutes.

4. Take the baking sheet out of the oven and stir the cauliflower around then bake for another 10 minutes.

5. Remove from the oven and allow to cool.

6. Into a large mixing bowl, add cooled cauliflower and all of the remaining ingredients. Mix well.

7. Allow mixture to sit for a minimum of 5 minutes.

8. Using gloved hands, spread the cauliflower dough onto a parchment-lined baking sheet or pizza pan. Bake for 22 minutes.

9. Remove from oven, flip the pizza crust over and cook for another 10 minutes.

10. Take out the crust and flip back to original side (with the crust shape). It should look like the picture at right. Add any sauce or toppings.

11. Increase the oven temperature to 400° and place the topped pizza back into the oven. Bake at 400° for 15-20 minutes. Watch for a golden brown on your cheese.

TIPS

- Start flattening the dough into a pizza shape beginning in the middle and pushing out towards the edge. This will help to make the shape of a crust easier.

- If you want to use a larger head of cauliflower, which might yield about 7 cups of riced cauliflower, and will make a thicker crust, it will need a bit more time baking in steps 8 and 9 to dry out and become firm. You may need about 1 Tbsp more of gluten-free all-purpose flour as well depending on the consistency of the dough.

Desserts

Not Just any Ole' Vanilla Cake with Lemon Vanilla Buttercream
Apple Pie
Pie Crust/Pastry Dough
"Our" Chocolate Chip Pecan Cookies
Double Dose of Chocolate Brownies
Fluffy Peanut Butter Cake
More Than A Simple Cheesecake
Nut Crust for Cookie Cheesecake
Powdered Sugar (Turbinado)
CinnaDoodle Cookie
Peanut Butter Cheesecake Brownies
Carrot Pecan Cake

Not Just any Ole' Vanilla Cake With Lemon Vanilla Buttercream

This light and airy cake is a lemony heaven! Topping the cake with lemon zest brings a magnificent pop of tartness that is complemented by the sweetness of the buttercream frosting.

PREP TIME: *20 minutes*   BAKE TIME: *38-40 minutes*   OVEN TEMP: *350°*
TOOLS: *(2) 8 inch cake rounds or (3) 6 inch cake rounds*

INGREDIENTS

Vanilla Cake:
1 tsp xanthan gum
¾ cup brown rice flour
¼ cup almond flour
¼ cup tiger nut flour
¼ cup sweet sorghum flour
¾ cup tapioca flour
1 tsp baking soda
2 tsp baking powder

1 tsp salt
1 ¼ cups raw cane sugar
⅔ cups mayonnaise
1 ½ tsp vanilla extract
½ cup unsweetened vanilla
   almond milk
½ cup warm water
4 eggs, room temperature

Lemon Vanilla Buttercream:
½ cup unsalted butter, cold
2 cups confectioners' sugar
2 Tbsp almond milk, cold
½ tsp vanilla extract
½ tsp lemon extract (or 1 tsp
   lemon juice)
½ tsp lemon zest (for frosting)
1 tsp lemon zest (for topping)

DIRECTIONS

1. Grease and flour (2) 8 inch cake rounds or (3) 6 inch cake rounds. Tap out any extra flour.

2. Sift together the dry ingredients: xanthan gum, brown rice flour, almond flour, tiger nut flour, sweet sorghum flour, tapioca flour, baking soda, baking powder, and salt.

3. In a separate bowl, cream together sugar and mayonnaise. Add in the vanilla and mix.

4. Slowly add the sugar mixture to the dry ingredients, alternating with the almond milk. Mix.

5. Add the water to the mixture. Mix.

6. Add one egg at a time. Mix a little bit in between.

7. Scrape the sides of the bowl to ensure all the ingredients are well combined.

8. Evenly distribute the batter into (2) 8 inch cake rounds, baking for 25-30 minutes or (3) 6 inch cake rounds, baking for 38-40 minutes.

9. Allow to cool thoroughly before frosting.

10. Frosting: Whisk all frosting ingredients together until smooth. Spread with a frosting knife or use a piping bag. Sprinkle 1 tsp lemon zest on top.

Apple Pie

INGREDIENTS

1 Gluten-Free Pie Crust (page 151)
6 cups apples cored, peeled, and cut (3 gala and 3 granny smith)
3 Tbsp unsalted butter

¼ cup packed brown sugar
1 Tbsp lemon juice
2 Tbsp Gluten-Free All-Purpose Flour blend (page 77)

1 teaspoon cinnamon
¼ teaspoon nutmeg

DIRECTIONS

1. Prepare a pie crust (page 151). Roll out crust and transfer to a 9 inch pie dish. Blind bake at 350° for 12 minutes. Set the second crust aside.

2. Core, peel, and cut the apples. Slice thin and then cut into bite sized cubes.

3. Into a medium pot add apples, lemon juice, and butter and cook covered over medium heat for 5 minutes.

4. Remove apple mixture from heat. Add sugar, cinnamon, nutmeg, and gluten-free all-purpose flour to the apple mixture. Mix well.

5. Pour apple mixture into the blind baked crust.

6. Roll out a second crust to place on top (see Tips for an alternative crumble recipe). Make a small slit in the crust for venting.

7. Bake the covered pie at 350° for 35-40 minutes.

TIPS

- Make this easy crumble to top your pie — then you can use the other half of your pastry dough for something else!

Crumble Topping:

½ cup pecan pieces
1 cup rolled oats (certified gluten-free)
1 tsp cinnamon
⅛ teaspoon nutmeg
¼ cup Gluten-Free All-Purpose Flour blend (page 77)
½ cup brown sugar
3-4 Tbsp cold butter, diced

1. Place the above ingredients in a food processor and blitz until it forms small bits. Oats and pecans should be smaller pieces but not fully ground. If you don't want to place butter in the food processor you can cut the butter into small bits and mix in the other ingredients by hand.

2. Sprinkle crumble mixture on top of the apples. Optional: Add additional 2 Tbsp butter on top of whole mixture.

3. Bake according to the recipe.

Pie Crust/Pastry Dough

PREP TIME: 25-30 minutes   *BAKE TIME: 12 minutes*   *OVEN TEMP: 350°*
MAKES: 2 crusts for a 9 inch pie dish

INGREDIENTS

2 ½ cups Gluten-Free All-
  Purpose Flour blend (page 77)
4 tsp sugar
¼ tsp fine salt

14 Tbsp cold butter, diced
1 large egg, lightly beaten with
  2 Tbsp cold water (put an ice
  cube in to keep really cold)

DIRECTIONS

1. Choose which method you will use, food processor, by hand, or both.
2. Cut butter into small cubes.
3. **By Hand:** In a medium bowl, whisk together the flour, sugar, and salt. Using your fingers, work the butter into the dry ingredients until it resembles pea-sized bits of butter. (If the flour/butter mixture gets warm, refrigerate it for 10 minutes before proceeding.) Add the egg/water mixture and mix into the dough using a fork or by hand. If the dough is dry, sprinkle up to a tablespoon more of cold water into the mixture.
   In A Food Processor: Use the grating attachment on your food processor and grate 14 Tbsp of frozen butter. If you don't have a grate attachment, cut cold butter into pieces. Pulse butter with the flour, sugar, and salt. Pulse about 10 times or just until combined — it should resemble pea-sized pieces. Add the egg/water mixture and pulse several more times until blended. Don't let the dough form into a ball in the machine. Dump dough onto the surface and work it together by hand. If the dough is dry, sprinkle up to a tablespoon more of cold water into the mixture.
4. Form the dough into a disk, wrap in plastic wrap and refrigerate until thoroughly chilled, at least 1 hour.
5. Cut the dough in ½ and roll out one half out as evenly as possible.
6. **If Blind Baking**: Place the rolled dough into a pie dish (if you have pie weights, place parchment paper on top of the dough and pour pie weights on top). Bake at 350° for 10-12 minutes.

TIPS

- Try not to overwork this pie crust in the hand stage so it can form layers and become flaky and puff up. I tend to start with the food processor and then gently work the dough with my hands.

- **Tip for rolling out your dough:** Take two long sheets of parchment paper — both long enough to hang over the side of the counter vertically. Dust one sheet of parchment with flour. Place dough in the middle and cover with the second piece of parchment paper, with the end hanging over the counter, vertically. Hold the paper down with your hip, or leg and roll. It provides the perfect tension for an awesomely even pie crust. Gently peel back one side and place your rolled out dough into the pie dish.

"Our" Chocolate Chip Pecan Cookies

Do you want to taste the chocolate chip cookie of your dreams? Childhood memories come flooding back with these cookies. My family likes the added kick the pecan gives, but this cookie stands on its own without the nuts!

PREP TIME: 6 minutes   **BAKE TIME:** 12-16 minutes   **OVEN TEMP:** 350°   **MAKES:** 30-36 cookies

INGREDIENTS

¾ cup butter, softened
¼ cup cane sugar
1 ¼ cup packed brown sugar
1 egg
1 tsp pure vanilla extract

½ cup tapioca flour
2 cups brown rice four
1 tsp xanthan gum
1 tsp baking soda
1 tsp baking powder

1 tsp salt
1 ½ cups chocolate chips
Optional: ½ cup pecans (if omitting, increase chocolate chips to 2 cups)

DIRECTIONS

1. In a stand mixer or using beaters, cream butter and sugars together on high for at least 1 minute.

2. Add egg and vanilla, mix.

3. Sift together tapioca flour, brown rice flour, xanthan gum, baking soda, baking powder, and salt.

4. Add the dry ingredients to the bowl and mix until smooth.

5. Add chocolate chips and optional nuts. Mix together.

6. Form 1 inch balls of dough and place 2 inches apart on parchment-lined baking sheets. Dough will be firm, pat down the dough balls just a little to flatten slightly.

7. Bake at 350° for 12 minutes for 1 inch dough balls, or 14-16 minutes for 2 inch dough balls.

TIPS

- Always make sure your dough is cold! You may need to pop it back into the refrigerator to cool off before baking, otherwise you will get a flat cookie.

- If you'd like to use salted butter for this recipe, you can reduce the salt to ½ tsp.

- Play with the flours: You can make this recipe with 1 cup white rice flour, 1 cup brown rice flour, and ½ cup tapioca flour.

- Can double the xanthan gum to 2 tsp and omit the baking soda if you don't have it on hand for a fluffy, cake-like cookie.

TWEAKS

_____

_____

Double Dose Of Chocolate Brownies

PREP TIME: 20 minutes   BAKE TIME: 30-35 minutes   OVEN TEMP: 350°   TOOLS: 9x13 inch baking dish

INGREDIENTS

1 cup softened unsalted butter
1 ½ cup cane sugar
1 tsp vanilla extract
3 eggs
1 cup Gluten-Free All-Purpose
  Flour blend (page 77)

½ cup cacao powder
¼ cup unsweetened cocoa powder
1 tsp baking powder
½ tsp baking soda
½ tsp salt

1 cup milk chocolate chips
½ cup 53% Cacao dark chocolate
  morsels chips

DIRECTIONS

1. Grease a 9x13 inch baking dish with butter, set aside.

2. Cream together butter and sugar.

3. Add vanilla and eggs. Mix.

4. In a separate bowl sift together flour, cacao powder, cocoa powder, baking powder, baking soda, and salt.

5. Add half the dry mixture to the butter mixture, at little a time, incorporating well before adding more.

6. Add chocolate chips.

7. Pour into greased baking dish. Use a spatula to spread batter evenly in the dish.

8. Bake at 350° for 30-35 minutes. Cool completely before trying to cut!

TWEAKS

_____

_____

_____

_____

_____

Fluffy Peanut Butter Cake with a Chocolate Twist

A long time ago, gluten-free cake wasn't an easy thing to come by. It was hard to find a cake that tasted the same as everyone else's "gluten-full" cakes. I came up with a basic chocolate and vanilla cake and have tweaked those recipes even further through the years. I swirled the two together for a third layer. These layers coupled with these two frostings makes this cake taste just like the famous sandwich combo I remember from my youth! Do you remember the combination of Fluff and peanut butter goodness to make the magical Fluffernutter? That combo was first born in 1914 by a woman named Emma Curtis, who thought of pairing of peanut butter with her and her brother's Snowflake Marshmallow cream!

PREP TIME: 10 minutes   **BAKE TIME: 30-38 minutes**   **OVEN TEMP: 350°**
TOOLS: (2) 8 inch cake rounds or (3) 6 inch cake rounds

INGREDIENTS

Cake:
2 ¼ cups Gluten-Free All-Purpose Flour blend (page 77)
⅔ cups mayonnaise
1 tsp baking soda
2 tsp baking powder
1 tsp salt
1 ½ tsp pure vanilla extract
3 eggs, room temperature
1 ½ cups cane sugar
1 cup + 4 Tbsp almond milk (or milk), divided
½ cup unsweetened cocoa powder

Vanilla Whipped Cream Frosting (the Fluff):
2 cups (1 pint) heavy whipping cream
1 cup +2 Tbsp confectioners sugar
1 tsp pure vanilla extract
2 tsp unflavored gelatin

Chocolate Peanut Butter Buttercream Frosting:
½ cup unsalted butter, softened
¼ cup cocoa powder, unsweetened
¼ tsp salt
1 ½ cup confectioners sugar
¼ cup smooth peanut butter (not the natural but the one with sugar)

TIPS

- If you want to make this an all-vanilla cake, omit step 6.
- If you want to make this an all-chocolate cake, add ½ cup cocoa powder and ½ cup almond milk to the batter. Add milk slowly until you have the consistency of cake batter.
- When making whipped cream frosting, I take a gel ice pack and place it under the bowl as I whip to keep the ingredients cold.

DIRECTIONS

1. Grease and flour (2) 8 inch cake rounds or (3) 6 inch cake rounds. Tap out any extra flour.

2. Sift together the dry ingredients: flour blend, baking soda, baking powder, and salt.

3. In a separate bowl, cream together sugar and mayonnaise. Add in the vanilla and mix.

4. Slowly add the sugar mixture to the dry ingredients, alternating with 1 cup of the almond milk.

5. Next add one egg at a time. Mix a little bit in between.

6. Divide the batter evenly into two bowls. Into one of the bowls add 4 Tbsp of almond milk and the unsweetened cocoa powder. Mix.

7. Scrape the sides of the bowls to ensure all the ingredients are well combined.

8. Evenly distribute the batter into (2) 8 inch cake rounds, baking for 25-30 minutes or (3) 6 inch cake rounds, baking for 32-38 minutes. If pouring into (3) 6 inch cake rounds, swirl the middle round by adding half vanilla batter and half chocolate batter, then use a butter knife and lightly swirl the two batters together.

9. Allow to cool thoroughly before frosting. Trim the top of the cake for layering the cakes evenly.

10. Make the Fluff: Mix all Vanilla Whipped Cream Frosting ingredients together with a whisk. Whip until stiff peaks form, about 5-8 minutes.

11. Make the Peanut Butter: Using a whisk, mix all Chocolate Peanut Butter Buttercream Frosting ingredients together until smooth and creamy looking. About 3-4 minutes.

More Than A Simple Cheesecake

There is lots of fun to be had with an awesome cheesecake, making this a great recipe to play around with! I added cookies which makes this cheesecake a winner in my family, but this recipe is great even without the cookies.

PREP TIME: *20 minutes*   **BAKE TIME:** *55-60 minutes*   **OVEN TEMP:** *325°*   **TOOLS:** *9 inch springform pan*

INGREDIENTS

1 Delectable Nut Crust
(page 160)
24 ounces (3 blocks) cream
cheese, room temperature

3 eggs, room temperature
1 tsp vanilla extract
1 cup cane sugar
12 vanilla creme sandwich cookies

DIRECTIONS

1. Prepare your crust: I used "Delectable Nut Crust" found on page 160.
2. In a stand mixer or using beaters, beat the cream cheese in a bowl until smooth and silky.
3. Add in eggs, one at a time, beating well after each addition and scraping down sides of the bowl as needed.
4. Add in sugar and vanilla and mix until the filling is super smooth.
5. Take your cookies and place them in a plastic zip-top bag then bang them with a meat hammer or a rolling pin into small/fine pieces.
6. Add the cookie crumbles to the batter and mix well.
7. Pour the batter into the pre-made crust and use a spatula to smooth out the top.
8. Place the pan onto a baking sheet then bake at 325° for 55-60 minutes. (See Tips.)
9. Allow to cool completely before refrigerating. Serve chilled.

TWEAKS

_____

_____

_____

_____

TIPS

- This recipe will still be delicious if you choose to use ⅓ less fat cream cheese but the full fat is a creamy masterpiece!

- The cheesecake is done when the top is ever so lightly browned yet firm all around the outside. The cake will still be set but have a very slight jiggle.

- Place the pan on a baking sheet to catch any drippings from the bottom of springform pan.

- Want a traditional cheesecake with a water bath? I often find I bake with less fuss, and according to my family's preferences. My family majority vote is a creamy (full fat) cake on the drier side, which tends to lend to slight cracking. While this may be my family's preference, I have done a water bath while baking a cheesecake and it comes out creamy and delectable! I wanted to include the water bath option so you can decide for yourself. Here is how I've done water baths for my cheesecakes:

  1. Boil about 5-6 cups of water.

  2. Take your prepared cheesecake in a springform pan and wrap the outside of the pan with a large piece of tin foil, avoiding touching the batter.

  3. Place the cake in a large roasting pan.

  4. Gently pour the boiled water into the roasting pan up to the middle of the springform pan.

  5. Bake for 1 hour-1 hour 10 minutes. Look for the set with a small jiggle!

Nut Crust for Cookie Cheesecake

This crust is so tasty I could eat it all by itself!

PREP TIME: 5 minutes   *BAKE TIME: 10 minutes*   *OVEN TEMP: 350°*   *TOOLS: 9 inch springform pan*

INGREDIENTS

1 cup raw almonds
1 cup raw cashews

5 Tbsp unsalted butter, divided
6 vanilla creme sandwich cookies

DIRECTIONS

1. Melt 4 Tbsp of butter (I use the microwave).
2. Add nuts and cookies to a food processor. Blitz until very small and crumbly.
3. Place nut/cookie mixture into a medium-sized bowl. Pour in the melted butter and mix well.
4. Use 1 Tbsp of butter to grease the the bottom and about 1-2 inches of the sides of the springform pan.
5. Pat the mixture firmly into the bottom and up the sides of the pan, using a small piece of wax paper or parchment paper to keep it from sticking to your hands.
6. Bake at 350° for 10 minutes.

Powdered Sugar (Turbinado)

PREP TIME: 5 minutes   *TOOLS: Vitamix or food processor*

INGREDIENTS

2 cups turbinado sugar

DIRECTIONS

1. Use a powerful blender or food processor and blitz the sugar. Watch the sugar pulverize from the bottom to the top. When it reaches the top and looks uniformly the same "lighter" color, stop.

TIPS

- This sugar will make a darker looking frosting, light brown in color. It brings a deep rich flavor with wonderful hints of molasses.

CinnaDoodle Cookies

I need to put a warning on this recipe: You will love these cookies so much that you will place them in the freezer to make them last. But sorry, this will not help because this airy and light cookie is even yummier when frozen! You were warned!

PREP TIME: 25 minutes   **BAKE TIME:** 14-15 minutes   **OVEN TEMP:** 375°   **MAKES:** 12 large cookies

INGREDIENTS

Batter Ingredients:
1 cup brown rice flour
1 cup white rice flour
1 cup tapioca flour
2 tsp xanthan gum
1 ¼ tsp ground cinnamon
½ tsp baking soda
1 tsp baking powder
1 cup salted butter
½ cup cane sugar
¼ cup packed light brown sugar
2 tsp vanilla extract
2 large eggs room temperature

Cinna Topping:
2 tsp ground cinnamon
3 Tbsp sugar

Frosting Ingredients:
2 ½ cups powdered sugar
5 Tbsp unsalted butter, room temperature
5 ounces cream cheese, room temperature
1 tsp vanilla extract
¼-½ Tbsp cold water, half and half, or milk

DIRECTIONS

1. Into a large mixing bowl, sift together brown rice flour, white rice flour, tapioca flour, xanthan gum, cinnamon, baking soda, and baking powder.

2. Using a stand mixer or beaters, cream together butter and both sugars until smooth and creamy.

3. Add one egg at a time to the butter mixture as you lightly mix.

4. Add the vanilla. Mix.

5. Add the dry mixture ⅓ at a time while mixing in between. Don't over mix, you are just trying to ensure it incorporates well. The dough should be light and airy.

6. Separate the dough into 12 equal sized balls.

7. Mix together the sugar and cinnamon for the Cinna Topping in a shallow dish or small bowl. Set aside.

8. Roll each dough ball in the Cinna Topping until fully covered then place onto a parchment-lined baking sheet. Lightly pat the ball down so it doesn't roll but do not flatten them. About 6 cookies will fit per sheet.

9. Bake at 375° for 14-15 minutes.

10. Cool them on a cooling rack.

11. While they are cooling make the frosting: Whisk together the powdered sugar, unsalted butter, cream cheese, vanilla and cold water, half and half, or milk. Note: You may not need the ¼-½ Tbsp of liquid to get a smooth frosting, so drizzle only a little in at a time.

TIPS

- Try switching from powdered sugar to powdered turbinado sugar. The powdered turbinado sugar makes a frosting with a deep, rich flavor. You will love the molasses notes from the turbinado!

- If you're using unsalted butter add ½ tsp salt to the cookie batter.

TWEAKS

_____

_____

_____

_____

_____

Cookies made from powdered sugar (left) and powdered sugar (turbinado) (right).

Peanut Butter Cheesecake Brownies

PREP TIME: 25 minutes   BAKE TIME: 55-60 minutes   OVEN TEMP: 350°   TOOLS: 9x13 inch baking dish

INGREDIENTS

- 1 batch Double Dose of Chocolate Brownie batter (page 155), unbaked
- 8 ounces cream cheese, room temperature
- 2 ½ cups powdered sugar
- 1 egg, room temperature
- 1 tsp vanilla extract
- ½ cup unsweetened natural smooth peanut butter
- ½ cup milk chocolate chips

DIRECTIONS

1. Grease a 9x13 inch baking dish with butter.
2. In a bowl, mix cream cheese, sugar, vanilla, egg, and peanut butter until smooth.
3. Pour the prepared brownie batter (page 155) into the bottom of the baking dish and smooth down.
4. Pour the cream cheese mixture on top of the brownie batter.
5. With a spatula or a spoon, swirl the cream cheese mixture into the brownie batter.
6. Sprinkle chocolate chips on top.
7. Bake at 350° for 40 minutes. After 40 minutes, place a piece of tin foil on top (to prevent burning) and bake for an additional 15 minutes.

TIPS

- Do you want to make this recipe but you only have sweetened peanut butter? Simply adjust the powdered sugar to ¾ cup and you are all set!
- For the absolute best tasting results allow these brownies to cool thoroughly. If you refrigerate this brownie and serve it cold, it's next level delicious!

Carrot Pecan Cake

PREP TIME: 20-25 minutes   *BAKE TIME: 30-48 minutes*   *OVEN TEMP: 350°*
TOOLS: (2) 9 inch cake rounds or (1) 8 cup Bundt cake pan

INGREDIENTS

Cake:
3 cups grated carrots (about 4
  large carrots)
2 cups Gluten-Free All-Purpose
  Flour blend (page 77)
1 ½ tsp baking soda
2 tsp cinnamon
½ tsp salt
1 ¼ cup extra virgin olive oil
1 cup raw sugar
1 cup packed brown sugar
1 tsp vanilla extract
4 large eggs, room temperature
1 cup pecans, chopped

Cream Cheese Frosting (as seen on cupcakes):
8 ounces cream cheese
2 tsp vanilla extract
1 ½ cups powdered sugar
⅓ cup + 1 Tbsp heavy whipping
  cream

Sour Cream Drizzle (as seen on bundt cake):
1 cup powdered sugar
4 ounces sour cream
1 tsp vanilla extract
Carrot zest

DIRECTIONS

1. Grease and flour (2) 9 inch cake rounds or (1) 8 cup Bundt cake pan. Tap out any extra flour.

2. Peel and grate the carrots.

3. Sift together the flour, baking soda, cinnamon, and salt.

4. In a separate bowl, mix together the olive oil and sugars. Add in the vanilla and carrots and mix.

5. Slowly add the dry ingredients to the carrot mixture, alternating with the eggs, one at a time. Mix only until batter is smooth, do not over mix.

6. Next add one egg at a time. Mix a little bit in between.

7. Scrape the sides of the bowl to insure all the ingredients are well combined.

8. Evenly distribute the batter into (2) 9 inch cake rounds, baking for 35-38 minutes, or into (1) 8 cup Bundt cake pan for 52-55 minutes. (I used a 6 cup Bundt cake pan so that I could have fun with cupcakes. If you want to do the same, bake the Bundt for 45-48 min and bake the cupcakes for 30-33 minutes.)

9. Cool completely before frosting!

10. Make the frosting, either Cream Chese Frosting, or Sour Cream Drizzle:

    Cream Cheese Frosting: Whisk together all ingredients until smooth.

    Sour Cream Drizzle: Mix all ingredients together then drizzle over cake.

    Top the cake with carrot zest.

Cakes for the Fluffy Peanut Butter Chocolate Cake before stacking (above).
The Fluffy Peanut Butter Chocolate Cake stacked and frosted (right).

About The Author

Jen lives in Georgia with her husband and two goldendoodles. She loves taking walks with her pups, visiting small towns throughout Georgia, hiking, and painting angels and nature scenes. She loves to cook for her husband, but looks forward to the times her adult children come home so they can enjoy all the family favorite recipes together with lots of laughter and story-telling.

To see the segments of Jen and her recipes on
local news channels or to contact her:

www.jenfiore.com

For more recipes, reviews on Jen's favorite gluten-free products, and tips Jen is sharing on:

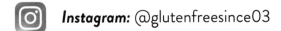 *Instagram:* @glutenfreesince03

Youtube: GlutenFree and Me

Facebook: https://www.facebook.com/jenfioreauthor/

TikTok: @glutenfreesince03

Notes

Notes